D0881871

REVERED WISDOM:
.....................................................

CHRISTIANITY
......................................

REVERED WISDOM

# CHRISTIANITY

## STERLING INNOVATION
An imprint of Sterling Publishing Co., Inc.

New York / London
www.sterlingpublishing.com

STERLING, the Sterling logo, STERLING INNOVATION, and the Sterling Innovation logo are registered trademarks of Sterling Publishing Co., Inc.

Library of Congress Cataloging-in-Publication Data Available

10  9  8  7  6  5  4  3  2  1

The text in this book is an abridged version of *Evidences of Christianity* by William Paley, originally published in 1851.

Published by Sterling Publishing Co., Inc.
387 Park Avenue South, New York, NY 10016

Distributed in Canada by Sterling Publishing
*c/o* Canadian Manda Group, 165 Dufferin Street
Toronto, Ontario, Canada M6K 3H6

Distributed in the United Kingdom by GMC Distribution Services
Castle Place, 166 High Street, Lewes, East Sussex, England BN7 1XU

Distributed in Australia by Capricorn Link (Australia) Pty. Ltd.
P.O. Box 704, Windsor, NSW 2756, Australia

*Printed in Singapore*

Design by Barbara Balch

Sterling ISBN 978-1-4027-7041-8

For information about custom editions, special sales, premium and corporate purchases, please contact Sterling Special Sales Department at 800-805-5489 or specialsales@sterlingpublishing.com.

# CONTENTS

........................

*Proposition II*

PART II:

*Of the Auxiliary Evidences of Christianity*

PART III:

*A Brief Consideration of Some Popular Objections*

# PREPATORY CONSIDERATIONS

I deem it unnecessary to prove that mankind stood in need of a revelation because I have met with no serious person who thinks that we have any degree of assurance which is superfluous. In judging of Christianity, the question lies between this religion and none: for, if the Christian religion be not credible, no one will support the pretensions of any other.

Suppose the world to have had a Creator; suppose that the Deity consulted for the happiness of his creation; suppose a part of the creation to have received faculties from their Maker, by which they are capable of a moral obedience to his will, and of voluntarily pursuing any end for which he has designed them; suppose the Creator to intend for these a second state of existence, in which their situation will be by their behaviour in the first state; suppose it to be of the utmost importance to the subjects of this dispensation to know what is intended for them, that the knowledge of it to be highly conducive to the happiness of the species: Suppose, nevertheless, almost the whole race to want this knowledge, and not to be likely, without the aid of a revelation, to attain it; under these circumstances, is it improbable that a revelation should be made?

Now in what way can a revelation be made, but by miracles? In none which we are able to conceive. Therefore, when miracles are related to have been wrought in the promulgating of a revelation manifestly wanted, the improbability which arises from the miraculous nature of the things related is not greater than the original improbability that such a revelation should be imparted by God.

We assert only, that in miracles adduced in support of revelation there is not any such antecedent improbability as no testimony can surmount. We contend that the incredibility of miracles related to have been wrought in attestation of a message from God, conveying intelligence of a future state of rewards and punishments, is not in itself greater than the event of the two following propositions being true: first, that a future state of existence should be destined by God for his human creation; and, secondly, that he should acquaint them with it. It is not necessary for our purpose, that these propositions be capable of proof; it is enough that they are not so violently improbable that either the propositions or facts strictly connected with the propositions, ought to be rejected, and to be rejected by whatever strength or of evidence they be attested.

If there be a revelation, there must be miracles, and, under the circumstances in which the human species are placed, a revelation is not improbable to be a fair answer to the whole objection.

But since it is an objection which stands in the very threshold our argument, and, if admitted, is a bar to every proof, it may be necessary to examine the principle upon which it professes to be founded; which is, that it is contrary to experience that a miracle should be true, but not contrary to experience that testimony should be false.

Now there appears a small ambiguity in the term "experience," and in the phrase, "contrary to experience." Strictly speaking, the narrative of a fact is then only contrary to experience, when the fact is related to have existed at a time and place, at which time and place we being present did not perceive it to exist. I know no intelligible signification which can be affixed to the term "contrary to experience," but one, viz., that of not having ourselves experienced anything similar to the thing related, or such things not being generally experienced by others.

Now the improbability which arises from the want of experience, is only equal to the probability there is, that, if the thing were true, we should experience things similar to it, or that such things would be generally experienced. Suppose it then to be true that miracles were wrought on the first promulgation of Christianity, is it certain that such miracles would be repeated so often as to become objects of general experience? And yet this probability is the exact converse, and therefore the exact measure, of the improbability which arises from the want of experience, and which Mr. Hume represents as invincible by human testimony.

To expect, concerning a miracle, that it should succeed upon a repetition, is to expect that which would make it cease to be a miracle and would totally destroy the use and purpose for which it was wrought.

The force of experience as an objection to miracles is founded in the presumption, either that the course of nature is invariable, or that variations will be frequent and general. Permit us to call the course of nature the agency of an intelligent Being. Ought we not to expect that such a Being, on occasions of peculiar importance, may interrupt the order which he had appointed, yet, that such occasions should return seldom; that these interruptions consequently should be confined to the experience of a few; that the want of it, therefore, in many, should be matter neither of surprise nor objection?

But it is said that, when we advance accounts of miracles, we assign effects without causes, or we attribute effects to causes inadequate to the purpose, or to causes of the operation of which we have no experience of what causes, we may ask, and of what effects, does the objection speak? If it be answered that, when we ascribe the cure of the palsy to a touch, of blindness to the anointing of the eyes with clay, or the raising of the dead to a word, we lay ourselves open to this imputation; we reply that we ascribe no such effects to such causes. They are merely signs to connect the miracle with its end. The effect we ascribe simply to the volition of Deity; of whose existence and power, we have previous and independent proof. Once believe that there is a God, and miracles are not incredible.

Mr. Hume states the ease of miracles to be a contest of opposite improbabilities. But herein I remark a want of argumentative justice, that, in describing the improbability of miracles, he suppresses all those circumstances of extenuation, which result from our knowledge of the existence, power, and disposition of the Deity; his concern in the creation, the end answered by the miracle, the importance of that end, and its subserviency to the plan pursued in the work of nature. As Mr. Hume has represented the question, miracles are alike incredible to him who is previously assured of the constant agency of a Divine Being, and to him who believes that no such Being exists in the universe. This surely cannot be a correct statement. In adjusting also the other side of the balance, the strength and weight of testimony, this author has provided an answer to every possible accumulation of historical proof by telling us that we are not obliged to explain how the story of the evidence arose. Now I think that we are obliged; by a probable hypothesis how it might so happen. The existence of the testimony is a phenomenon; the truth of the fact solves the phenomenon. If we reject this solution, we ought to have some other to rest in.

But the short consideration which convinces me that there is no solid foundation in Mr. Hume's conclusion, is the following. If twelve men, whose probity and good sense I had long known, should seriously relate to me an account of a miracle wrought before their eyes, and in which it was impossible that they should be deceived: if the governor of the country, hearing a rumour of this account, should call these men and offer them either to confess the imposture, or submit to be tied up to a gibbet; if they should refuse to acknowledge any falsehood in the case: if it was at last executed; if I myself saw them consenting to be racked, burnt, or strangled, rather than live up the truth of their account;—still if Mr. Hume's rule be my guide, I am not to believe them. Now I undertake to say that there exists not a sceptic in the world who would not believe them.

Instances of spurious miracles supported by strong testimony undoubtedly demand examination; Mr. Hume has endeavoured to fortify his argument by some examples of this kind. I hope to show that none of them reach the strength or circumstances of the Christian evidence.

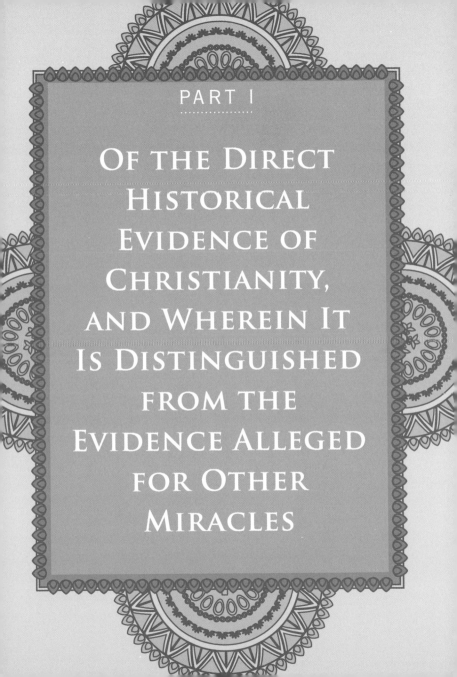

# PART I

# OF THE DIRECT HISTORICAL EVIDENCE OF CHRISTIANITY, AND WHEREIN IT IS DISTINGUISHED FROM THE EVIDENCE ALLEGED FOR OTHER MIRACLES

The two propositions which I shall endeavour to establish are these:

1. That there is satisfactory evidence that many professing to be original witnesses of the Christian miracles passed their lives in labours, dangers, and sufferings, voluntarily undergone in attestation of the accounts which they delivered, and solely in consequence of their belief of those accounts; and that they also submitted, from the same motives, to new rules of conduct.

2. That there is not satisfactory evidence that persons professing to be original witnesses of other miracles, in their nature as certain as these are, have ever acted in the same manner, in attestation of the accounts which they delivered, and properly in consequence of their belief of those accounts.

# PROPOSITION I

## CHAPTER I

## EVIDENCE OF THE SUFFERING OF THE FIRST PROPAGATORS OF CHRISTIANITY, FROM THE NATURE OF THE CASE

To support this first proposition, two points are necessary to be made out: first, that the Founder of the institution, his associates and immediate followers, acted the part which the proposition imputes to them: secondly, that they did so in attestation of the miraculous history recorded in our Scriptures, and solely in consequence of their belief of the truth of this history.

It will be proper to consider the degree of probability which the assertion derives from the nature of the case.

First, then, the Christian Religion exists, and, therefore, was established. Now it either owes its establishment to the activity of the Person who was the founder of the institution, and of those who were joined with him in the undertaking, or that, although they might lie by, others would take it up. To me it appears certain, that, if the first announcing of the religion by the Founder had not been followed up by the zeal and industry of his immediate disciples, the attempt must have expired in its birth. Then as to the mode of life to which these persons submitted, we reasonably suppose it to be like that which we observe in all others who voluntarily become missionaries of a new faith. Frequent, earnest, and laborious preaching, constantly conversing with religious persons upon religion, a sequestration from the common pleasures, engagements, and varieties of life, and an addiction to one serious object, compose the habits of such men. Very few hypocrites engage in these undertakings; or persist in them long. Ordinarily speaking, nothing can overcome the indolence of mankind, the love of cheerful society, or the desire of personal ease and freedom, but conviction.

Secondly, it is also highly probable, that the propagation of the new religion was attended with difficulty and danger. As addressed to the Jews, it was a system adverse to those opinions upon which their hopes, their partialities, their pride, their consolation, was founded. This people had worked themselves into a persuasion, that some signal and greatly advantageous change was to be effected in the condition of their country, by the agency of a long-promised messenger from heaven.* The rulers of the Jews had been the authors of this persuasion. So that it was not merely the conjecture of theoretical divines, but it was become the popular hope and Passion, and undoubting and impatient of contradiction. To find, therefore, that expectations so gratifying were to end in the diffusion of a mild unambitious religion, which, instead of exalting their nation and institution above the rest of the world, was to advance those whom they despised, could be no very pleasing discovery; nor could the messengers of such intelligence expect to be well received or easily credited. The doctrine was equally harsh and novel. The extending of the kingdom of God to those who did not conform to the law of Moses was a notion that had never before entered into the thoughts of a Jew.

The character of the new institution was ungrateful to Jewish habits and principles. Their own religion was in a high degree technical. Even the enlightened Jew placed a great deal of stress upon the ceremonies of his law. The Christian scheme, without formally repealing the Levitical code, lowered its estimation extremely. In the place of strictness and zeal in performing the observances which that code

---

* "Pererebuerat oriento toto vetus et contans opinio, esse in fatis, ut eo tempore Judaea profecti rerum potirsatur." Sueton. Vespasian. cap. 4–8.

"Pluribus persuasio inerat, antiquis sacerdotum literis contineri, eo ipso tempore fore, ut valesecret oriens, profectique Judaea rerum potirentur." Tacit. Hist. lib. v. cap. 9–13.

prescribed, the new sect preached up faith, well-regulated affections, inward purity, and moral rectitude of disposition, as the true ground of merit and acceptance with God. This did not by any means facilitate the plan then.

The ruling party at Jerusalem had just before crucified the Founder of the religion. They, therefore, who stood forth to preach the religion must necessarily reproach these rulers with an execution which they could not but represent as a murder. This would not render their office more easy, or their situation more safe.

With regard to the interference of the Roman government which was then established in Judea, despising as it did the religion of the country, it would, if left to itself, animadvert upon the schisms and controversies which arose within it. Yet there was that in Christianity which might easily afford a handle of accusation with a jealous government. The Christians avowed an unqualified obedience to a new master. They avowed also that he was the person who had been foretold to the Jews under the title of King. The spiritual nature of this kingdom, the consistency of this obedience with civil subjection, were distinctions too refined to be entertained by a Roman president. Our histories accordingly inform us, that this was the turn which the enemies of Jesus gave to his character and pretensions in their remonstrances with Pontius Pilate. And it was undoubtedly a natural source of calumny and misconstruction.

The preachers of Christianity had, therefore, to contend with prejudice backed by power. They had to come forward to a disappointed people, to a priesthood possessing municipal authority, and actuated by strong motives of opposition and resentment; and they had to do this under a foreign government. The fate of reformers will not allow us to suppose that the first propagators of Christianity at Jerusalem and in Judea, entirely destitute as they were of force, authority, or protection, could execute their mission with personal ease and safety.

Let us next inquire, what might reasonably be expected by the preachers of Christianity when they turned themselves to the heathen public. The religion they carried with them was exclusive. It denied the truth of every article of heathen mythology. It accepted no compromise, it admitted no comprehension. It must prevail by the overthrow of every statue, altar, and temple in the world. It will not easily be credited, that a design, so bold as this was, could be attempted to be carried into execution with impunity.

For it ought to be considered, that this was not some new competitor for a place in the Pantheon, without questioning the reality of any others: it was pronouncing all other gods to be false, and all other worship vain

It ought also to be considered, that this was not philosophers propounding doubts concerning the truth of the popular creed, or even avowing their disbelief of it. These philosophers did not go about from place to place to form societies professing their tenets; to provide for the order, instruction and permanency of these societies; nor did they enjoin their followers to withdraw themselves from the public worship of the temples, or refuse a compliance with rites instituted by the laws.* These things are what the Christians did; and in these consisted the activity and danger of the enterprise.

Thirdly, it ought also to be considered, that this danger proceeded from sudden bursts of violence at particular places, from the licence of the populace, the rashness of some magistrates and negligence of others; from the instigation of interested adversaries, and from the variety and warmth of opinion which an errand so novel and extraordinary could not fail of exciting. The teachers of Christianity might both fear and suffer much from these causes, without any general persecution being denounced against them by imperial authority. Some length of time might pass, before the vast machine of the Roman empire would be put in motion: but, during that time, a great deal of ill usage might be endured, by a set of friendless, unprotected travellers, telling men, wherever they came, that the religion of their ancestors, the religion of the state, was a system of folly and delusion.

The truth is, the ancient heathens considered religion entirely as an affair of state, as much under the tuition of the

---

* Plato, Cicero, and Epictetus enjoined men to worship the gods of the country, and in the established form. See passages to this purpose collected from their works by Dr. Clarke, Nat. and Rev. Rel. p. 180. ed. v—Except Socrates, they all thought it wiser to comply with the laws than to contend.

magistrate as any other part of the police. The religion of that age was not merely allied to the state; it was incorporated into it. Many of its offices were administered by the magistrate. Without discussing, therefore, the truth of the theology, they resented every affront put upon the established worship, as a direct opposition to the authority of government.

Add to which, that the religious systems of those times had been long established. The ancient religion of a country has always many votaries because its origin is hidden in remoteness and obscurity. Men have a natural veneration for antiquity, especially in matters of religion. What Tacitus says of the Jewish was more applicable to the heathen establishment: "Hi ritus, quoquo modo inducti, antiquitate defenduntur." It was also a sumptuous worship. It had its priesthood, its endowments, its temples. Statuary, painting, architecture, and music, contributed their effect to its ornament and magnificence. It abounded in festival shows and solemnities, to which the common people are greatly addicted. These things would retain great numbers on its side by the fascination of spectacle and pomp, as well as interest many in its preservation by the advantage which they drew from it. On the due celebration also of its rites, the people did believe that the prosperity of their country in a great measure depended.

I am willing to accept the account which is given by Mr. Gibbon: "The various modes of worship which prevailed in the Roman world were all considered by the people as equally true, by the philosopher as equally false, and by the magistrate as equally useful:" And I would ask from which of these three classes were the Christian missionaries to look for protection or impunity? Could they expect it from the people, "whose acknowledged confidence in the public religion" they subverted from its foundation? From the philosopher, who, "considering all religious as equally false," would of course rank theirs among the number? Or from the magistrate, who, satisfied with the "utility" of the subsisting religion, would not be likely to countenance a spirit of proselytism and innovation:—a system which declared war against every other, and which, if it prevailed, must end in a total rupture of public opinion; an upstart religion which was not content with its own authority, but must disgrace all the settled religions of the world? It was not to be imagined that he would endure with patience.

Lastly; the nature of the case affords a strong proof, that the original teachers of Christianity, in consequence of their new profession, entered upon a new and singular course of life. The institution which they preached to others, they conformed to in their own persons; because this is no more than what every teacher of a new religion must do, in order to obtain either proselytes or hearers. The change which this would produce was very considerable. After men became Christians, much of their time was spent in prayer and devotion, in religious meetings, in celebrating the Eucharist, in conferences, in exhortations, in preaching, in an affectionate intercourse with one another, and correspondence with other societies. How new! What a revolution there must have been of opinions and prejudices to bring the matter to this!

We know what the precepts of the religion are. We are entitled to contend, that the observable part of their behaviour must have agreed with the duties which they taught. There was, therefore, a course of life pursued by them, different from that which they before led. And this is of great importance. Men are brought to anything almost sooner than to change their habit of life, especially when the change is made against the force of natural inclination. It is the most difficult of all things to convert men from vicious habits to virtuous ones.* It is almost like making men over again.

---

* Hartley's *Essays on Man*, p. 190.

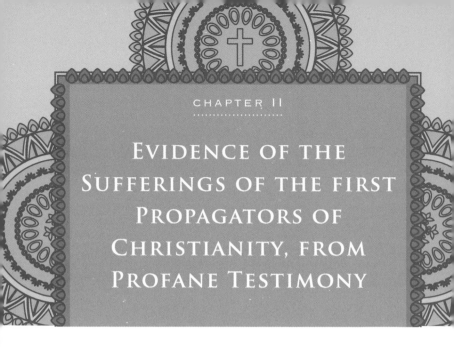

# EVIDENCE OF THE SUFFERINGS OF THE FIRST PROPAGATORS OF CHRISTIANITY, FROM PROFANE TESTIMONY

After thus considering what was likely to happen, we are next to inquire how the transaction is represented in the several accounts that have come down to us.

The obscure view of Christianity, which some of the heathen writers of that age had gained offers itself to our notice: because it is the concession of adversaries; the source from which it is drawn is unsuspected. A quotation from Tacitus must be inserted, as deserving particular attention. This passage was written about seventy years after Christ's death, and it relates to transactions which took place about thirty years after that event—Speaking of the fire which happened at Rome in the time of Nero, and of the suspicions that the emperor himself was concerned in causing it:—

"But neither these exertions, nor his largesses to the people, nor his offerings to the gods, did away the infamous imputation under which Nero lay, of having ordered the city to be set on fire. To put an end, therefore, to this report, he laid the guilt, and inflicted the most cruel punishments, upon a set of people, who were holden in abhorrence for their crimes, and called by the vulgar, Christians. The founder of that name was Christ, who suffered death in the reign of Tiberius, under his procurator, Pontius Pilate— This pernicious superstition, thus checked for a while, broke out again; and spread not only over Judea, where the evil originated, but through Rome also, whither everything bad upon the earth finds its way and is practised. Some who confessed their sect were first seized, and afterwards, by their information, a vast multitude were apprehended, who were convicted, not so much of the crime of burning Rome, as of hatred to mankind. Their sufferings at their execution were aggravated by insult and mockery; for some were disguised in the skins of wild beasts, and worried to death by dogs; some were crucified; and others were wrapped in pitched shirts,* and set on fire when the day closed, that they might serve as lights to illuminate the night. Nero lent his own gardens for these executions, and exhibited at the

---

* This is rather a paraphrase, but is justified by what the Scholiast upon Juvenal says; "Nero maleficos homines taeda et papyro et cera supervestiebat, et sic ad ignem admoveri jubebat." Lard. Jewish and Heath. Test. vol. i. p. 359.

same time a mock Circensian entertainment; being a spectator of the whole, in the dress of a charioteer, sometimes mingling with the crowd on foot, and sometimes viewing the spectacle from his car. This conduct made the sufferers pitied; and though they were criminals, and deserving the severest punishments, yet they were considered as sacrificed, not so much out of a regard to the public good, as to gratify the cruelty of one man."

Our concern with this passage is only as it affords a presumption in support of the proposition which we maintain. Now, considered in this view, it proves three things: 1st, that the Founder of the institution was put to death; 2dly, that in the same country in which he was put to death, the religion, after a short check, broke out again and spread; 3dly, that it so spread as that, within thirty-four years from the Author's death, a very great number of Christians were found at Rome. From which fact, the two following inferences may be drawn: first, that if, in the space of thirty-four years, the religion had extended itself to Rome, and there had numbered a great multitude of converts, the original teachers and missionaries of the institution could not have been idle; secondly, that when the Author of the undertaking was put to death, the endeavours of his followers to establish his religion in the same country, amongst the same people, and in the same age, could not but be attended with danger.

Suetonius, a writer contemporary with Tacitus, describing the same reign, uses these words: "Affecti suppliciis

Christiani genus hominum superstitionis novae et malefi-
cae." (Suet. Nero. Cap. 16) "The Christians, a set of men of
a new and mischievous superstition, were punished."

Since it is not mentioned here that the burning of the
city was the pretence of the punishment of the Christians,
it is probable that Suetonius refers to some more general
persecution than the short one which Tacitus describes.

Juvenal, a writer of the same age, and intending to
commemorate the cruelties exercised under Nero's government, has the following lines: (Sat. i. ver. 155)

"Describe Tigellinus (a creature of Nero), and you shall
suffer the same punishment with those who stand burning
in their own flame and smoke, their head being held up by
a stake fixed to their chin, till they make a long stream of
blood and melted sulphur on the ground."

These things took place within thirty-one years after
Christ's death, in the life-time, probably, of some of the
apostles, and certainly in the life-time of those who were
converted by the apostles. If then the Founder of the religion was put to death; if the first race of converts to the religion suffered the greatest extremities for their profession; it
is hardly credible, that those who were companions of the
Author of the institution during his life, and the teachers
and propagators of the institution after his death, could go
about their undertaking with ease and safety.

The testimony of the younger Pliny is confined to the
affairs of his own time. His letter to Trajan was written about
seventy years after Christ's death; and the information to

be drawn from it relates to two points: first, to the number of Christians in Bithynia and Pontus, which was so considerable as to induce the governor of these provinces to speak of them: "There are many of every age and of both sexes;— nor has the contagion of this superstition seized cities only, but smaller towns also, and the open country." Great exertions must have been used by the preachers of Christianity to produce this state of things within this time. Secondly, the sufferings to which Christians were exposed, without any public persecution being denounced against them by sovereign authority. For, from Pliny's doubt how he was to act, requesting the emperor's rescript, and the emperor propounding a rule for his direction without reference to any prior rule, it may be inferred that there was, at that time, no public edict in force against the Christians. Yet from this same epistle of Pliny it appears "that accusations, trials, and examinations, were, and had been, going on against them in the provinces over which he presided; that schedules were delivered by anonymous informers, containing the names of persons who were suspected of holding or of favouring the religion; that, in consequence of these informations, many had been apprehended, of whom some boldly avowed their profession, and died in the cause; others denied that they were Christians; others, acknowledging that they had once been Christians, declared that they had long ceased to be such." All which demonstrates that Christianity was at that time attended with fear and danger: and yet this took place without any edict from the Roman sovereign. This observation is further confirmed by a rescript of Adrian to Minucius Fundanus, the proconsul of Asia (Lard. Heath. Test. vol. ii. p. 110): from which it appears that the custom of the people of Asia was to proceed against the Christians with tumult and uproar. This disorderly practice is recognised in the edict, because the emperor enjoins, that if the Christians were guilty, they should be legally brought to trial, and not be pursued by importunity and clamour.

Martial wrote a few years before the younger Pliny: and made the suffering of the Christians the subject of his ridicule.

> *In matutina nuper spectatus arena*
> *Mucius, imposuit qui sua membra focis,*
> *Si patiens fortisque tibi durusque videtur,*
> *Abderitanae pectora plebis habes;*
> *Nam cum dicatur, tunica praesente molesta,*
> *Ure\* manum: plus est dicere, Non facio.*

Martial's testimony, as well indeed as Pliny's, goes also to another point that the deaths of these men were martyrdom in the strictest sense.

The constancy of the Christians of this period, is also referred to by Epictetus, who imputes their intrepidity to madness, or to a kind of habit; and about fifty years afterwards, by Marcus Aurelius, who ascribes it to obstinacy.

---

*Forsan "thure manum."

# INDIRECT EVIDENCE OF THE SUFFERINGS OF THE FIRST PROPAGATORS OF CHRISTIANITY, FROM THE SCRIPTURES AND OTHER ANCIENT CHRISTIAN WRITINGS

Of the primitive condition of Christianity, a distant only view can be acquired from heathen writers. It is in our own books that the detail must be sought for. Now these books come up in their accounts to the full extent of the proposition which we maintain. We have four histories of Jesus Christ. We have a history taking up the narrative from his death, and carrying on an account of the propagation of the religion, for a space of nearly thirty years. We have a collection of letters, written by certain principal agents in the business upon the business, and in the midst of their concern and connection with it. And we have these writings severally attesting the sufferings of the witnesses of the history.

I may be allowed therefore, to suggest some conclusions of this sort, as preparatory to more direct testimony.

1. Our books relate, that Jesus Christ, the founder of the religion, was, in consequence of his undertaking, put to death at Jerusalem. This point is no more than what Tacitus has recorded. They then proceed to tell us that the religion was set forth at this same city of Jerusalem, propagated thence throughout Judea, and afterwards preached in other parts of the Roman Empire. These points also are fully confirmed by Tacitus. What could the disciples of Christ expect for themselves when they saw their master put to death? With this example before their eyes, they could not be without a full sense of the peril of their future enterprise.

2. Secondly, all the histories agree in representing Christ as foretelling the persecution of his followers:—

> "Then shall they deliver you up to be afflicted, and shall kill you, and ye shall be hated of all nations for my name's sake." (Matt. xxiv. 9.)

> "When affliction or persecution ariseth for the word's sake, immediately they are offended." (Mark iv. 17. See also chap. x. 30.)

> "They shall lay hands on you, and persecute you, delivering you up to the synagogues, and

into prisons, being brought before kings and rulers for my name's sake:—and ye shall be betrayed both by parents and brethren, and kinsfolks and friends, and some of you shall they cause to be put to death." (Luke xxi. 12–16. See also chap. xi. 49.)

I am not entitled to argue that Christ actually did foretell these events, and that they did accordingly come to pass; because that would be at once to assume the truth of the religion: but I am entitled to contend that one side or other of the following disjunction is true; either that the Evangelists have delivered what Christ really spoke, and that the event corresponded with the prediction; or that they put the prediction into Christ's mouth, because the event had turned out so to be: for, the only two remaining suppositions appear in the highest degree incredible; which are, either that Christ filled the minds of his followers with fears, without any reason for what he said; or that, although Christ had never foretold any such thing, yet historians who lived in the age when the event was known, falsely, as well as officiously, ascribed these words to him.

3. Thirdly, these books abound with exhortations to patience.

"Who shall separate us from the love of Christ? Shall tribulation, or distress, or persecution, or famine, or nakedness, or peril, or sword? Nay, in all these things we are more than conquerors through Him that loved us." (Rom. viii. 35–37.)

"We are troubled on every side, yet not distressed; we are perplexed, but not in despair; persecuted, but not forsaken; cast down, but not destroyed; always bearing about in the body the dying of the Lord Jesus, that the life also of Jesus might be made manifest in our body;—knowing that he which raised up the Lord Jesus shall raise us up also by Jesus, and shall present us with you—For which cause we faint not; but, though our outward man perish, yet the inward man is renewed day by day. For our light affliction, which is but for a moment, worketh for us a far more exceeding and eternal weight of glory." (2 Cor. iv. 8, 9, 10, 14, 16, 17.)

"So that we ourselves glory in you in the churches of God, for your patience and faith in all your persecutions and tribulations that ye endure. Which is a manifest token of the righteous judgment of God, that ye may be counted worthy of the kingdom for which ye also suffer." (2 Thess. i. 4, 5.)

"We rejoice in hope of the glory of God; and not only so, but we glory in tribulations also; knowing that tribulation worketh patience, and patience experience, and experience hope." (Rom. v. 3, 4.)

What could all these texts mean, if there was nothing in the circumstances of the times which required patience? Or will it be pretended, that these exhortations were put in merely to induce a belief in after-ages, that the Christians underwent sufferings which they did not undergo? If these books belong to the age to which they lay claim, and in which age they certainly did appear, this supposition cannot be maintained; because I think it impossible to believe that passages, which must be deemed false, by the persons into whose hands the books upon their publication were to come, should nevertheless be inserted, for the purpose of producing an effect upon remote generations. In forgeries which do not appear till many ages after that to which they pretend to belong, it is possible that some contrivance of that sort may take place; but in no others can it be attempted.

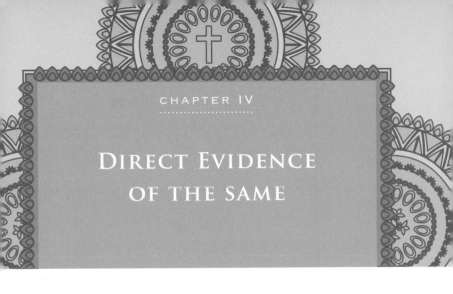

## CHAPTER IV

# DIRECT EVIDENCE
# OF THE SAME

The account of the treatment of the religion, and of the exertions of its first preachers, as stated in our Scriptures, is the following: "That the Founder of Christianity, from the commencement of his ministry to the time of his violent death, employed himself wholly in publishing the institution in Judea and Galilee; that, in order to assist him in this purpose, he made choice, out of the number of his followers, of twelve persons, who might accompany him as he travelled from place to place; that, except a short absence upon a journey in which he sent them two by two to announce his mission, and one of a few days, when they went before him to Jerusalem, these persons were steadily and constantly attending upon him; that they were with him at Jerusalem when he was apprehended and put to death; and that they were commissioned by him, when his own ministry was concluded, to publish his Gospel, and collect disciples to it from all countries of the world." The account then proceeds to state, "that a few days after his departure, these persons, with some of his relations, and some who had regularly frequented their society, assembled at Jerusalem; that, considering the office of preaching the religion as now devolved upon them, and one of their number having deserted the cause, and, repenting of his perfidy, having destroyed himself, they proceeded to elect another into his place, and that they were careful to make their election out of the number of those who had accompanied their master from the first to the last, in order, as they alleged, that he might be a witness, together with themselves, of the principal facts which they were about to produce and relate concerning him; (Acts i. 12, 22.) that they began their work at Jerusalem by publicly asserting that this Jesus, whom the rulers and inhabitants of that place had so lately crucified, was, in truth, the person in whom all their prophecies and long expectations terminated; that he had been sent amongst them by God; and that he was appointed by God the future judge of the human species; that all who were solicitous to secure to themselves happiness after death, ought to receive him as such, and to make profession of their belief, by being baptised in his name." (Acts xi.)

The history goes on to relate, "that considerable numbers accepted this proposal, and that they who did so formed amongst themselves a strict union and society; (Acts iv. 32.)

that the attention of the Jewish government being soon drawn upon them, two of the principal persons of the twelve, and who also had lived most intimately and constantly with the Founder of the religion, were seized as they were discoursing to the people in the temple; that after being kept all night in prison, they were brought the next day before an assembly composed of the chief persons of the Jewish magistracy and priesthood; that this assembly, after some consultation, found nothing, at that time, better to be done towards suppressing the growth of the sect, than to threaten their prisoners with punishment if they persisted; that these men, after expressing, in decent but firm language, the obligation under which they considered themselves to be, to declare what they knew, 'to speak the things which they had seen and heard,' returned from the council, and reported what had passed to their companions; that this report, whilst it apprized them of the danger of their situation and undertaking, had no other effect upon their conduct than to produce in them a general resolution to persevere, and an earnest prayer to God to furnish them with assistance, and to inspire them with fortitude, proportioned to the increasing exigency of the service." (Acts iv.) A very short time after this, we read "that all the twelve apostles were seized and cast into prison; (Acts v. 18.) that, being brought a second time before the Jewish Sanhedrim, they were upbraided with their disobedience to the injunction which had been laid upon them, and beaten for their contumacy; that, being charged once more to desist, they were suffered to depart; that however they neither quitted

Jerusalem, nor ceased from preaching, both daily in the temple, and from house to house (Acts v. 42.) and that the twelve considered themselves as so entirely and exclusively devoted to this office, that they now transferred what may be called the temporal affairs of the society to other hands."*

Hitherto the preachers of the new religion seem to have had the common people on their side; which is assigned as the reason why the Jewish rulers did not, at this time, proceed to greater extremities. It was not long, however, before the enemies of the institution found means to represent it to the people as tending to subvert their law, degrade their lawgiver, and dishonour their temple. (Acts vi. 12.) And these insinuations were dispersed as to induce the people to join with their superiors in the stoning of a very active member of the new community.

The death of this man was the signal of a general persecution, which may be judged of from one anecdote of the time:—"As for Saul, he made havoc of the church, entering

---

* I do not know that it has ever been insinuated that the Christian mission, in the hands of the apostles, was a scheme for making a fortune. But it may nevertheless be fit to remark how perfectly free they appear to have been from any pecuniary or interested views whatever. The most tempting opportunity which occurred of making gain of their converts, was by the custody and management of the public funds. Yet, so undesirous were they of the advantage which that confidence afforded, that we find they very soon disposed of the trust, by putting it into the hands of stewards formally elected for the purpose by the society at large.

into every house, and taking men and women committed them to prison." (Acts viii. 3.) This persecution raged at Jerusalem with so much fury as to drive most of the new converts out of the place,* except the twelve apostles. The converts thus "scattered abroad," preached the religion wherever they came; and their preaching was, in effect, the preaching of the twelve; for it was so far carried on in correspondence with them, that when they heard of the success in a particular country, they sent two of their number to the place, to complete the mission.

An event now took place, of great importance in the future history of the religion. The persecution which had begun at Jerusalem followed the Christians to other cities, (Acts ix.) in which the authority of the Jewish Sanhedrim over those of their own nation was allowed to be exercised. A young man, who had procured a commission to seize any converted Jews whom he might find at Damascus, suddenly became a proselyte to the religion which he was going about to extirpate. The new convert not only shared, on this extraordinary change, the fate of his companions, but brought upon himself a double measure of enmity from the party which he had left. The Jews at Damascus watched the gates with so much diligence, that he escaped only by

---

*Acts viii. I. "And they were all scattered abroad;" but the term "all" is not, I think, to be taken strictly as denoting more than the generality; in like manner as in Acts ix. 35: "And all that dwelt at Lydda and Saron saw him, and turned to the Lord."

being let down in a basket by the wall. Nor did he find himself in greater safety at Jerusalem. Attempts were there also soon set on foot to destroy him; from the danger of which he was preserved by being sent away to Cilicia.

For some reason not mentioned, an intermission about this time took place in the sufferings of the Christians. This happened, only seven or eight, perhaps only three or four years after Christ's death, within which period, churches had been formed in all Judea, Galilee, and Samaria; for we read that the churches in these countries "had now rest and were edified, and, walking in the fear of the Lord, and in the comfort of the Holy Ghost, were multiplied." (Acts ix 31.) The original preachers of the religion did not remit their labours during this season of quietness; for we find one passing throughout all quarters. We find also those who had been before expelled from Jerusalem, travelling as far as Poenice, Cyprus, and Antioch; (Acts xi. 19.) and lastly, we find Jerusalem again in the centre of the mission.

The time of this tranquillity did not, however, continue long. Herod Agrippa, who had lately acceded to the government of Judea, "stretched forth his hand to vex certain of the church." (Acts xii. 1.) He began by beheading one of the twelve original apostles. He proceeded to seize, in order to put to death, another of the number. This man was, however, delivered from prison, as the account states miraculously, (Acts xii. 3–17.) and made his escape from Jerusalem.

These things are related with the utmost particularity of names, persons, places, and circumstances; and without the smallest discoverable propensity in the historian, to magnify the fortitude, or exaggerate the sufferings, of his party. When they fled for their lives, he tells us. When the churches had rest, he remarks it. When the apostles were carried a second time before the Sanhedrim, he is careful to observe that they were brought without violence. When the rulers contented themselves with threatening the apostles, and commanding them to be beaten with stripes, without urging at that time the persecution further, the historian candidly records their forbearance. When, therefore, in other instances, he states heavier persecutions, or actual martyrdoms, it is reasonable to believe that he states them because they were true.

Our history now pursues a narrower path. Leaving the rest of the apostles engaged in the propagation of the new faith, the narrative proceeds with the separate memoirs of that eminent teacher, whose extraordinary and sudden conversion to the religion had before been circumstantially described. This person, in conjunction with another, who appeared amongst the immediate adherents of the twelve apostles, (Acts iv. 36.) set out from Antioch upon the express business of carrying the new religion through the various provinces of the Lesser Asia. (Acts xiii. 2.) During this expedition, we find that in almost every place to which they came, their persons were insulted, and their lives endangered. After being expelled from Antioch, they repaired to

Iconium. (Acts xiii. 51.) At Iconium, an attempt was made to stone them; at Lystra, one of them actually was stoned and drawn out of the city for dead. (Acts xiv. 19.) These two men were acting in conjunction with the original apostles.

The treatment which they had experienced in the first progress did not deter them from preparing for a second. Upon a dispute, however, arising between them, each devoting his endeavours to the advancement of the religion, they parted from one another, and set forward upon separate routes. The history goes along with one of them; and the second enterprise to him was attended with the same dangers and persecutions as both had met with in the first. He now crosses for the first time the Aegean sea, and carries with him, amongst others, the person whose accounts supply the information we are stating. (Acts xvi. 11.) The first place in Greece at which he appears to have stopped, was Philippi in Macedonia. Here himself and one of his companions were cruelly whipped, cast into prison, and kept there under the most rigorous custody, being thrust, whilst yet smarting with their wounds, into the inner dungeon, and their feet made fast in the stocks. (Acts xvi. 23, 24, 33.) Notwithstanding this, they went forward. After passing through Amphipolis and Apollonia, they came to Thessalonica; in which city the house in which they lodged was assailed by a party of their enemies. And when they were not found at home, the master of the house was dragged before the magistrate. (Acts xvii. 1–5.) Their reception at the next city was better: but before long their turbulent adversaries the Jews, excited against them such commotions as obliged the apostle to make his escape by a private journey to Athens. (Acts xvii. 13.) The extremity of the progress was Corinth. His abode in this city, for some time, seems to have been without molestation. At length, however, the Jews found means to bring him before the tribunal of the Roman president. (Acts xviii. 12.) It was to the contempt which that magistrate entertained for the Jews and their controversies that our apostle owed his deliverance. (Acts xviii. 15.)

This indefatigable teacher again visited Jerusalem, which still continued the centre of the mission. (Acts xviii. 22.) We find him going thence to Antioch, and, traversing once more the northern provinces of Asia Minor. (Acts xviii. 23.) This progress ended at Ephesus: in which city, the apostle continued in the daily exercise of his ministry two years, and until his success excited the apprehensions of those who were interested in the national worship. Their clamour produced a tumult, in which he had nearly lost his life. (Acts xix. 1, 9, 10.) He was driven from Ephesus only to renew his labours in Greece. After passing over Macedonia, he thence proceeded to his former station at Corinth. (Acts xx. 1, 2.) He pursued his voyage with all the expedition he could command, in order to reach Jerusalem against the feast of Pentecost. (Acts xx. 16.) He had been only a few days in that city, when the populace, instigated by some of his old opponents in Asia, who attended this feast, seized him in the temple, and were ready immediately to have destroyed him, had not the sudden presence of the Roman guard rescued him out of their hands. (Acts xxi. 27–33.) The officer, however, who had thus seasonably interposed, acted from his care of the public peace, and not from any favour to the apostle; for he had no sooner secured his person in the fortress, than he was proceeding to examine him by torture. (Acts xxii 24.)

From this time to the conclusion of the history, the apostle remains in public custody of the Roman government. After delivering himself from the influence of his enemies by an appeal to the audience of the emperor, (Acts xxv. 9, 11.) he was sent, but not until he had suffered two years' imprisonment, to Rome. (Acts xxiv. 27.) He reached Italy after encountering in his passage the perils of a desperate shipwreck. (Acts xxvii.) The historian closes the account by telling us that, for two years, he received all that came unto him in his own hired house, where he was permitted to dwell with a soldier that guarded him, "preaching the kingdom of God, and teaching those things which concern the Lord Jesus Christ, with all confidence."

Now the historian, from whom we have drawn this account is supported by the strongest corroborating testimony. We are in possession of letters written by Saint Paul himself upon the subject of his ministry. These letters, without borrowing from the history, or the history from them, unintentionally confirm the account which the history delivers, in a great variety of particulars. What belongs to our present purpose is the description exhibited of the apostle's sufferings: and the representation, given in our history, not only agrees in general with the language which he himself uses, but is also, in many instances, attested by a specific correspondency of time, place, and order of events. If the historian put down in his narrative, that at Philippi the apostle "was beaten with many stripes, cast into prison, and there treated with rigour and indignity;" (Acts xvi. 23, 24.) we find him (I Thess. ii. 2.) reminding his converts that, "after he had suffered before, and was shamefully entreated at Philippi, he was bold, nevertheless, to speak unto them (to whose city he next came) the Gospel of God." If the history relates that, (Acts xvii. 5.) at Thessalonica, the house in which the apostle was lodged was assaulted by the populace, and the master of it dragged before the magistrate for admitting such a guest; the apostle, in his letter to the Christians of Thessalonica, calls to their remembrance "how they had received the Gospel in much affliction." (1 Thess. i. 6.) If the history deliver an account of an insurrection at Ephesus, which had nearly cost the apostle his life, we have the apostle himself describing his despair, and returning thanks for his deliverance. (Acts xix. 2 Cor. i. 8–10.) If the history inform us, that the apostle was expelled from Antioch in Pisidia, attempted to be stoned at Iconium, and actually stoned at Lystra; there is preserved a letter from him to a favourite convert; in which letter he appeals to that disciple's knowledge "of the persecutions which befell him at Antioch, at Iconium, at Lystra." (Acts xiii. 50; xiv. 5, 19. 2 Tim. 10, 11.)

These coincidences, together with many relative to other parts of the apostle's history, and all drawn from independent sources, not only confirm the truth of the account, but add much to the credit of the narrative in all its parts; and support the author's profession of being a contemporary of the person whose history he writes, and, throughout a material portion of his narrative, a companion.

What the epistles of the apostles declare of the suffering state of Christianity the writings which remain of their companions and immediate followers expressly confirm.

Clement, who is honourably mentioned by Saint Paul in his epistle to the Philippians, (Philipp. iv. 3.) hath left us his attestation to this point: "Let us take (says he) the examples of our own age. Through zeal and envy, the most faithful and righteous pillars of the church have been persecuted even to the most grievous deaths. Let us set before our eyes the holy apostles. Peter, by unjust envy, underwent not one or two, but many sufferings; till at last, being martyred, he went to the place of glory that was due unto him. For the same cause did Paul, in like manner, receive the reward of his patience. Seven times he was in bonds; he was whipped, was stoned; he preached both in the East and in the West, leaving behind him the glorious report of his faith; and so having taught the whole world righteousness, and for that end travelled even unto the utmost bounds of the West, he at last suffered martyrdom by the command of the governors, and departed out of the world, and went unto his holy place, being become a most eminent pattern of patience unto all ages. To these holy apostles were joined a very great number of others, who, having through envy undergone, in like manner, many pains and torments, have left a glorious example to us. For this, not only men, but women, have been persecuted; and, having suffered very grievous and cruel punishments, have finished the course of their faith with firmness." (Clem. ad Cor. c. v. vi. Abp. Wake's Trans.)

Hermas, saluted by Saint Paul in his epistle to the Romans, thus speaks: "Such as have believed and suffered death for the name of Christ, and have endured with a ready mind, and have given up their lives with all their hearts." (Shepherd of Hermas, c. xxviii.)

Polycarp, the disciple of John, has not left this subject unnoticed. "I exhort (says he) all of you, that ye obey the word of righteousness, and exercise all patience, which ye have seen set forth before your eyes, not only in the blessed Ignatius, and Lorimus, and Rufus, but in others among yourselves, and in Paul himself and the rest of the apostles; being confident in this, that all these have not run in vain, but in faith and righteousness; and are gone to the place that was due to them from the Lord, with whom also they suffered. For they loved not this present world, but him who died, and was raised again by God for us." (Pol. ad Phil c. ix.)

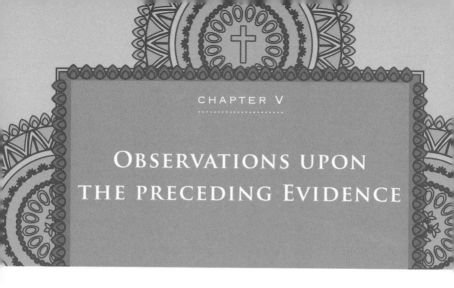

## CHAPTER V

# OBSERVATIONS UPON THE PRECEDING EVIDENCE

On the history, of which the last chapter contains an abstract, there are a few observations which it may be proper to make, by way of applying its testimony to the particular propositions for which we contend.

I. Although our Scripture history leaves the general account of the apostles in an early part of the narrative, and proceeds with the separate account of one particular apostle, the information extends to the rest, as it shows the nature of the service. When we see one apostle suffering persecution, we shall not believe, without evidence, that the same office could, at the same time, be attended with ease and safety to others. And this fair and reasonable inference is confirmed by the direct attestation of the letters, to which we have so often referred. "I think that God hath set forth us the apostles last, as it were, appointed to death; for we are made a spectacle unto the world, and to angels, and to men; even unto this present hour, we both hunger and thirst, and are naked, and are buffeted, and have no certain dwelling-place; and labour, working with our own hands: being reviled, we bless; being persecuted, we suffer it; being defamed, we entreat: we are made as the filth of the earth, and as the offscouring of all things unto this day." (I Cor. iv. 9, et seq.) Add to which, that in the short account that is given of the other apostles in the former part of the history, we find, first, two of them seized, imprisoned, brought before the Sanhedrim, and threatened with further punishment; (Acts iv. 3, 21.) then, the whole number imprisoned and beaten; (Acts v. 18, 40.) soon afterwards, one of their adherents stoned to death, and so hot a persecution raised against the sect as to drive most of them out of the place; one of the twelve was beheaded, and another sentenced to the same fate; and all this passing in the single city of Jerusalem, and within ten years after the Founder's death.

II. We take no credit at present for the miraculous part of the narrative, nor do we insist upon the correctness of single passages of it. If the whole story be not a novel; if Peter, and James, and Paul, and the rest of the apostles mentioned, be not all imaginary persons; if their letters be not all forgeries; then is there evidence in our hands sufficient to support that the original followers of Jesus Christ exerted great endeavours to propagate his religion, and underwent great labours, dangers, and sufferings, in consequence of their undertaking.

III. The general reality of the apostolic history is confirmed by the consideration, that it does no more than assign adequate causes for effects which were produced; and describe consequences naturally resulting from situations which existed. The effects were there, of which this history sets forth the cause, and origin, and progress. It is acknowledged because it is recorded by other testimony than that of the Christians themselves, that the religion began to prevail at that time, and in that country. It is very difficult to conceive how it could begin without the exertions of the Founder and his followers. It is admitted that the religion was adverse to the reigning opinions, and to the hopes and wishes of the nation to which it was first introduced; and that it overthrew, so far as it was received, the established theology and worship of every other country. We cannot feel much reluctance in believing that when the messengers of such a system went about not only publishing their opinions, but collecting proselytes, and forming regular societies of proselytes, they should meet with opposition in their attempts, or that this opposition should sometimes proceed to fatal extremities.

IV. The records before us supply evidence that, together with activity and courage in propagating the religion, the primitive followers of Jesus assumed, upon their conversion, a new and peculiar course of private life. Immediately after their Master was withdrawn from them, we hear of their "continuing with one accord in prayer and supplication;" (Acts i. 14.) of their "continuing daily with one accord in the temple" (Acts ii.

46.) Of "many being gathered together praying." (Acts xii. 12.) We know that strict instructions were laid upon the converts by their teachers. The first word of their preaching was, "Repent!" These injunctions obliged them to refrain from many species of licentiousness, which were not reputed criminal. We know the rules of purity, and of benevolence, which Christians read in their books; concerning which rules it is enough to observe, that, if they were, but in any degree regarded, they could produce a system of conduct, and, a disposition of mind, and a regulation of affections, different from anything to which they had hitherto been accustomed. The change and distinction of manners, which resulted from their new character, is perpetually referred to in the letters of their teachers. "And you hath he quickened, who were dead in trespasses and sins, wherein in times past ye walked, according to the course of this world, according to the prince of the power of the air, the Spirit that now worketh in the children of disobedience; among whom also we all had our conversation in times past, in the lusts of our flesh, fulfilling the desires of the flesh, and of the mind, and were by nature the children of wrath, even as others." (Eph. ii 1–3. See also Tit. iii. 3) Saint Paul, in his first letter to the Corinthians, after enumerating a catalogue of vicious characters, adds, "Such were some of you; but ye are washed, but ye are sanctified." (1 Cor. vi. 11.) The phrases which the same writer employs to describe the moral condition of Christians, compared with their condition before they became Christians, such as "newness of life," being "freed from sin," being "dead to sin;" "the destruction of the body of sin, that, for the future, they should not serve sin;" "children of light and of the day," as opposed to "children of darkness and of the night;" "not sleeping as others;" imply a new system of obligation, and, probably, a new series of conduct, commencing with their conversion.

The testimony which Pliny bears, and which comes not more than fifty years after that of St. Paul, is very applicable to the subject under consideration. The character which this writer gives of the Christians of that age is as follows:—He tells the emperor, "that some of those who had relinquished the society, or who, to save themselves, pretended that they had relinquished it, affirmed that they were wont to meet together on a stated day, before it was light, and sang among themselves alternately a hymn to Christ as a God; and to bind themselves by an oath, not to the commission of any wickedness, but that they would not be guilty of theft, or robbery, or adultery; that they would never falsify their word, or deny a pledge committed to them, when called upon to return it." This proves that a morality, more strict than was ordinary, prevailed at that time in Christian societies. And we are authorised to carry his testimony back to the age of the apostles; because it is not probable that the immediate disciples of Christ were more relaxed than their successors, or the missionaries of the religion than those whom they taught.

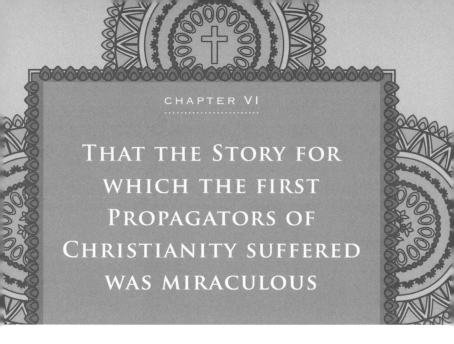

# THAT THE STORY FOR WHICH THE FIRST PROPAGATORS OF CHRISTIANITY SUFFERED WAS MIRACULOUS

When we consider, first, the prevalency of the religion at this hour; secondly, the only credible account which can be given of its origin; thirdly, the opposition which that activity must naturally have excited; fourthly, the fate of the Founder of the religion; fifthly, the testimony of writers to the sufferings of Christians; sixthly, predictions of the suffering of his followers ascribed to the Founder of the religion; seventhly, letters now in our possession, written by some of the principal agents in the transaction, referring expressly to extreme labours, dangers, and sufferings; lastly, a history purporting to be written by a fellow-traveller of one of the new teachers, and, by its unsophisticated correspondency with letters of that person still extant, proving itself to be written by some one well acquainted with the subject of the narrative: when we lay together these considerations, there cannot much doubt remain upon our minds but that a number of persons at that time appeared in the world, publicly advancing an extraordinary story, and for the sake of propagating the belief of that story, voluntarily incurring great personal dangers, traversing seas and kingdoms, exerting great industry, and sustaining great extremities of ill usage and persecution. It is also proved that the same persons, in consequence of their persuasion, of the truth of what they asserted, entered upon a course of life in many respects new and singular.

I think it to be likewise in the highest degree probable, that the story for which these persons voluntarily exposed themselves to the fatigues and hardships which they endured was a miraculous story. They had nothing else to stand upon. The designation of Jesus of Nazareth, rather than any other person, was the Messiah, and as such the subject of their ministry, could only be founded upon supernatural tokens attributed to him. A Galilean peasant was announced to the world as a divine lawgiver. A young man of mean condition, and who had wrought no deliverance for the Jewish nation, was declared to be their Messiah. This, without ascribing to him at the same time some proofs of his mission, was too absurd a claim to be either imagined, or attempted, or credited. In whatever degree the religion was argumentative, when it came to the question, "Is the carpenter's son of Nazareth the person whom we are to receive and obey?" there was nothing but the miracles attributed to him by which his pretensions could be maintained. Every controversy must presuppose these: for, however such controversies might and naturally would, be discussed upon their own grounds of argumentation, without citing the miraculous evidence, yet without previously supposing the existence or the pretence of such evidence, there could have been no place for the discussion of the argument at all. Thus, for example, whether the prophecies, which the Jews interpreted to belong to the Messiah, were or were not applicable to the history of Jesus of Nazareth, was a natural subject of debate in those times; and the debate would proceed without recurring at every turn to his miracles, because it set out with supposing these; inasmuch as without miraculous marks and tokens, I do not see how the question could ever have been entertained. Apollos, we read, "mightily convinced the Jews, showing by the Scriptures that Jesus was Christ;" (Acts xviii. 28.) but unless Jesus had exhibited some proof of supernatural power, the argument from the old Scriptures could have had no place. It had nothing to attach upon. A young man calling himself the Son of God, gathering a crowd about him, and delivering to them lectures of morality, could not have excited so much as a doubt among the Jews, whether he was the object in whom a long series of ancient prophecies terminated, from the completion of which they had formed such magnificent expectations of a nature so opposite to what appeared; I mean no such doubt could exist when they had the whole case before them, when they saw him put to death for his officiousness, and when by his death the evidence concerning him was closed. Again, the effect of the Messiah's coming, supposing Jesus to have been he, upon Jews, upon Gentiles, upon their relation to each other, upon their acceptance with God, upon their duties and their expectations; his nature, authority, office, and agency; were likely to become subjects of much consideration with the early votaries of the religion, and to occupy their attention and writings. I should not however expect, that in these disquisitions, frequent or very direct mention of his miracles would occur. Still, miraculous evidence lay at the bottom of the argument. In the primary question, miraculous pretensions alone, were what they had to rely upon.

That the original story was miraculous, is very fairly also inferred from the miraculous powers which were laid claim to by the Christians of succeeding ages. If the accounts of these miracles be true, it was a continuation of the same powers; if they be false, it was an imitation of what had been reported to have been wrought, by those who preceded them. That imitation should follow reality, if miracles were performed at first, miracles should be pretended afterwards; agrees so well with the ordinary course of human affairs, that we can have no great difficulty in believing it. The contrary supposition is very improbable.

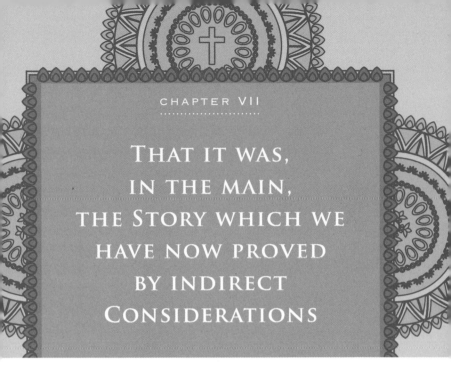

# THAT IT WAS, IN THE MAIN, THE STORY WHICH WE HAVE NOW PROVED BY INDIRECT CONSIDERATIONS

I t being then once proved, that the first propagators of the Christian institution did exert activity, and subject themselves to great dangers and sufferings, in consequence and for the sake of an extraordinary and a miraculous story; the next great question is, whether the account, which our Scriptures contain, be that story? This question is, in effect, whether the story which Christians have now be the story which Christians had then?

In the first place, there exists no trace or vestige of any other story. It is not a competition between opposite accounts, or between the credit of different historians. There is not a document, or scrap of account, which assigns a history substantially different from ours. The notices of the affair which are found in heathen writers go along with us. They go on, further, to describe the manners of Christians in terms perfectly conformable to the accounts extant in our books.

This is the account of writers who viewed the subject at a great distance; who were uninformed and uninterested about it. It bears the characters of such an account upon the face of it, because it describes the appearance in the world of a new religion, and the conversion of great multitudes to it, without descending to the detail of the transaction upon which it was founded, the interior of the institution, the evidence offered by those who drew over others to it. Yet still here is no contradiction of our story: but so far a confirmation of it as that, in the general points on which the heathen account touches, it agrees with that which we find in our own books.

The same may be observed of the very few Jewish writers of that and the adjoining period. They advance no other history of the transaction than that which we acknowledge. Josephus, who wrote his Antiquities, or History of the Jews, about sixty years after the commencement of Christianity, in a passage generally admitted as genuine, makes mention of John under the name of John the Baptist; that he was a preacher of virtue; that he baptized his proselytes; that he was well received by the people; that he was imprisoned and put to death by Herod. (Antiq. I. xviii. cap. v. sect. 1, 2.) In another passage allowed by many, we hear of "James, the brother of him who was called Jesus, and of his being put to death." (Antiq. I. xx. cap. ix. sect. 1.) In a third passage, extant in every copy that remains of Josephus's history, but the authenticity of which has nevertheless been long disputed, we have an explicit testimony to the substance of our history in these words:— "At that time lived Jesus, a wise man, if he may be called a man, for he performed many wonderful works. He was a teacher of such men as received the truth with pleasure. He drew over to him many Jews and Gentiles. This was the Christ; and when Pilate, at the instigation of the chief men among us had condemned him to the cross, they who before had conceived an affection for him did not cease to adhere to him; for, on the third day, he appeared to them alive again, the divine prophets having foretold these and many wonderful things concerning him. And the sect of the Christians, so called from him, subsists to this time." (Antiq. I. xviii. cap. iii. sect 3.)

But further; the whole series of Christian writers, from the first age of the institution down to the present, in their discussions, apologies, arguments, and controversies, proceed upon the general story which our Scriptures contain, and upon no other. This argument will appear to be of great force, when it is known that we are able to trace back the series of writers to a contact with the historical books of the New Testament, and to the age of the first emissaries of the religion, and to deduce it, by an unbroken continuation, from that end of the train to the present.

The remaining letters of the apostles incidentally disclose to us the following circumstances:—Christ's descent and family; his innocence; the meekness and gentleness of his character; his exalted nature; his circumcision; his transfiguration; his life of opposition and suffering; his patience and resignation; the appointment of the Eucharist; his agony; his confession before Pontius Pilate; his stripes, crucifixion, and burial; his resurrection; his ascension into heaven; and his designation to be the future judge of mankind; the stated residence of the apostles at Jerusalem; the working of miracles by the first preachers of the Gospel;* the successful propagation of the religion; the persecution of its followers; the miraculous conversion of Paul; miracles wrought by himself; finally, that MIRACLES were the signs of an apostle.[+]

In an epistle bearing the name of Barnabas, the companion of Paul, we have the sufferings of Christ, his choice

---

* Heb. ii. 3. "How shall we escape, if we neglect so great salvation, which, at the first, began to be spoken by the Lord, and was confirmed unto us by them that heard him, God also be bearing them witness, both with signs and wonders, and with divers miracles, and gifts of the Holy Ghost?" I allege this epistle without hesitation; for, whatever doubts may have been raised about its author, there can be none concerning the age in which it was written. No epistle in the collection carries about it more indubitable marks of antiquity than this does. It speaks for instance, throughout, of the temple as then standing and of the worship of the temple as then subsisting.—Heb. viii. 4: "For, if he were on earth, he should not be a priest, seeing there

of apostles and their number, his passion, the scarlet robe, the vinegar and gall, the mocking and piercing, the casting lots for his coat, (Ep. Bar. c. vii.) his resurrection on the eighth, his manifestation after his resurrection, and, lastly, his ascension. We have also his miracles generally referred to in the following words:—"Finally, teaching the people of Israel, and doing many wonders and signs among them, he preached to them, and showed the exceeding great love which he bare towards them." (Ep. Bar. c. v.)

In an epistle of Clement, a hearer of St. Paul, we have the resurrection of Christ, and the subsequent mission of the apostles: "The apostles have preached to us from our Lord Jesus Christ from God:—For, having received their command, and being thoroughly assured by the resurrection of our Lord Jesus Christ, they went abroad, publishing that the kingdom of God was at hand." (Ep. Clem. Rom. c. xlii.) We find noticed, also, the humility, yet the power of Christ, (Ep. Clem. Rom. c. xvi.) his descent from Abraham—his crucifixion. We have Peter and Paul represented as faithful and righteous pillars of the church; the numerous sufferings of Peter; the stoning of Paul, and more particularly his extensive and unwearied travels.

---

are priests that offer according to the law."—Again, Heb. xiii. 10: "We have an altar whereof they have no right to eat which serve the tabernacle."

+ Truly the signs of as apostle were wraught among you in all patience, in signs, and wonders, and mighty deeds. 2 Cor. xii. 12.

In an epistle of Polycarp, a disciple of St. John, though only a brief hortatory letter, we have the humility, patience, sufferings, resurrection, and ascension of Christ, together with the apostolic character of St. Paul, distinctly recognised. (Pol. Ep. Ad Phil. C. v. viii. ii. iii.) Of this same father we are also assured, by Irenaeus, that he (Irenaeus) had heard him relate, "what he had received from eye-witnesses concerning the Lord, both concerning his miracles and his doctrine." (Ir. ad Flor. 1 ap. Euseb. l. v. c. 20.)

In the remaining works of Ignatius, larger than those of Polycarp, the occasional allusions are proportionably more numerous. The descent of Christ from David, his mother Mary, his miraculous conception, the star at his birth, his baptism by John, his appeal to the prophets, the ointment poured on his head, his sufferings under Pontius Pilate and Herod the tetrarch, his resurrection, the Lord's day called and kept in commemoration of it, and the Eucharist, in both its Parts,—are unequivocally referred to. Upon the resurrection, this writer is even circumstantial. He mentions the apostles' eating and drinking with Christ after he had risen, their feeling and their handling him; from which last circumstance Ignatius raises this just reflection;—They believed, being convinced both by his flesh and spirit; for this cause, they despised death, and were found to be above it." (Ad Smyr. c. iii.)

Quadratus, of the same age with Ignatius, has left us the following noble testimony:—"The works of our Saviour were always conspicuous, for they were real; both those that were healed, and those that were raised from the dead; who were seen not only when they were healed or raised, but for a long time afterwards; not only whilst he dwelled on this earth, but also after his departure, and for a good while after it, insomuch that some of them have reached to our times." (Ap. Euseb. H. E. l. iv. c. 3.)

Justin Martyr came little more than thirty years after Quadratus. From Justin's works, which are still extant, might be collected a tolerably complete account of Christ's life, in all points agreeing with that which is delivered in our Scriptures; taken indeed, in a great measure, from those Scriptures, but still proving that this account was the account extant in that age. The miracles in particular stand fully and distinctly recognised:—"He healed those who had been blind, and deaf, and lame from their birth; causing, by his word, one to leap, another to hear, and a third to see: and, by raising the dead, and making them to live, he induced, by his works, the men of that age to know him." (Just. Dial. cum Tryph. p. 288, ed. Thirl.)

It is unnecessary to carry these citations lower, because the history, after this time, occurs in ancient Christian writings as familiarly as it is wont to do in modern sermons.

This is not only true of those writings of Christians which are of acknowledged authority; but it is, in a great measure, true of all their ancient writings which remain. Whatever fables they have mixed with the narrative, they preserve the material parts, the leading facts, as we have them; and, so far as they do this, they are evidence that these points were fixed, were acknowledged by all Christians in the ages in which the books were written

Now that the original story delivered by the first preachers, should have died away so entirely as to have left no record, although so many records of the time and transaction remain; and that another story should have gained exclusive possession of the belief of all who professed, themselves disciples of the institution, is beyond any example of the corruption of even oral tradition, and still less consistent with the experience of written history: and this improbability is rendered still greater by the reflection, that no such oblivion of one story, and the substitution of another, took place in any future period of the Christian aera. Christianity hath travelled through dark and turbulent ages; nevertheless it came out in substance, as it entered in.

Thirdly: The religious rites and usages that prevailed amongst the early disciples of Christianity sprung out of the narrative now in our hands; which accordancy shows, that it was the narrative which they had received from their teachers. Our account makes the Founder of the religion direct that his disciples should be baptized: we know that the first Christians were baptized. Our account makes him direct that they should hold religious assemblies: we find that they did. Our accounts make the apostles assemble upon a stated day of the week: the Christians of the first century did observe stated days of assembling. Our histories record the institution of the rite which we call the Lord's Supper, and a command to repeat it in perpetual succession: we find, amongst the early Christians, the celebration of this rite universal. There is no room for insinuating that our books were fabricated with a studious accommodation to the usages which obtained at the time they were written. The Scripture accounts, especially of the Lord's Supper, are too short and cursory, not to say too obscure, and in this view, deficient, to allow a place for any such suspicion.*

Amongst the proofs of the truth of our proposition, it appears by the Gospels themselves that that the Christian community was already in possession of the substance and principal parts of the narrative. The Gospels were not the original cause of the Christian history being believed, but were themselves among the consequences of that belief. This is expressly affirmed by Saint Luke, in his preface:— "Forasmuch (says the evangelist) as many have taken in hand to set forth in order a declaration of those things which are most surely believed amongst us, even as they delivered them unto us, which, from the beginning, were eye-witnesses and ministers of the word; it seemed good to me also, having had perfect understanding of all things from the very first, to write unto thee in order, most excellent Theophilus, that

---

* The reader who is conversant in these researches, by comparing the short Scripture accounts of the Christian rites above-mentioned with the minute and circumstantial directions contained in the pretended apostolical constitutions, will see the force of this observation.

thou mightest know the certainty of those things wherein thou hast been instructed."—This short introduction testifies, that the substance of the history which the evangelist was about to write was already believed by Christians; that the office which the historian proposed to himself was to trace each particular to its origin, and to fix the certainty of many things which the reader had before heard of. In Saint John's Gospel the same point appears hence, that there are some principal facts to which the historian refers, but which he does not relate. A remarkable instance of this kind is the ascension, which is not mentioned by St. John in its place, but which is plainly referred to in the following words of the sixth chapter; "What and if ye shall see the Son of man ascend up where he was before?" (Also John iii. 31; and xvi. 28.) And still more positively in the words which Christ, according to our evangelist, spoke to Mary after his resurrection, "Touch me not, for I am not yet ascended to my Father: but go unto my brethren, and say unto them, I ascend unto my Father and your Father, unto my God and your God." (John xx. 17.) This can only be accounted for by the supposition that St. John wrote under a sense of the notoriety of Christ's ascension. The same account must also be given of Saint Matthew's omission of the same important fact. It agrees also with this solution, that neither Matthew nor John disposes of the person of our Lord in any manner whatever.

These four circumstances:—first, the recognition of the account in its principal parts by a series of succeeding writers; secondly, the total absence of any account of the origin of the religion substantially different from ours; thirdly, the early and extensive prevalence of rites and institutions, which resulted from our account; fourthly, our account bearing in its construction proof that it is an account of facts which were known and believed at the time, are sufficient to support an assurance, that the story which we have now is, in general, the story which Christians had at the beginning. I say in general; that it is the same in its principal facts.

And if our evidence stopped here, we should have a strong case to offer: for we should have to allege, that in the reign of Tiberius Caesar, a certain number of persons set about an attempt of establishing a new religion in the world: in the prosecution of which purpose, they voluntarily encountered great dangers, undertook great labours, sustained great sufferings, all for a miraculous story, which they published wherever they came; and that the resurrection of a dead man, whom during his life they had followed and accompanied, was a constant part of this story. I know nothing in the above statement which can, with any appearance of reason, be disputed; and I know nothing, in the history of the human species, similar to it.

## CHAPTER VIII

# THE SAME PROVED FROM THE AUTHORITY OF OUR HISTORICAL SCRIPTURES

Whether the historical books of the New Testament be deserving of credit as histories, is a point which necessarily depends upon what we know of the books, and of their authors.

Now, the first and most material observation is, that such was the situation of the authors to whom the four Gospels are ascribed, that, if any one of the four be genuine, it is sufficient for our purpose. The received author of the first was an original apostle and emissary of the religion. The received author of the second was an inhabitant of Jerusalem to whose house the apostles were wont to resort, and himself an attendant upon one of the most eminent of that number. The received author of the third was a stated companion and fellow-traveller of the most active of all the teachers of the religion, and frequently in the society of the original apostles. The received author of the fourth was one of these apostles. The authors of all the histories lived at the time and upon the spot. The authors of two of the histories were present at many of the scenes which they describe; writing from personal knowledge and recollection; and, writing upon a subject in which their minds were deeply engaged. Whoever reads the Gospels will find in them detailed circumstantial accounts of miracles, with specifications of time, place, and persons; and these accounts many and various. In the Gospels, therefore, which bear the names of Matthew and John, these narratives, if they really proceeded from these men, must either be true as far as the fidelity of human recollection is usually to be depended upon, or they must be wilful and mediated falsehoods. Yet the writers who fabricated these falsehoods, if they be such, are of the number of those who sacrificed their ease and safety in the cause, and for a purpose most inconsistent with dishonest intentions. They were villains for no end but to teach honesty, and martyrs without the least prospect of honour or advantage.

The Gospels which bear the names of Mark and Luke, although not the narratives of eye-witnesses, are, if genuine, removed from that only by one degree. They are the narratives of contemporary writers mixing with the business; one of the two probably living in the place which was the principal scene of action; both living in habits of society and correspondence with those who had been present at the transactions which they relate. The latter of them accordingly tells us that the things which were believed about Christians came from those who from the beginning were eye-witnesses and ministers of the word; that he had traced accounts up to their source; and that he was prepared to instruct his reader in the certainty of the things which he related.*

The situation of the writers applies to the truth of the facts which they record. But at present we use their testimony to a point somewhat short of this, namely, that the facts recorded in the Gospels are the facts which the original preachers of the religion allege. I am concerned only to show, that what the Gospels contain is the same as what the apostles preached. Now, how stands the proof of this point? A set of men went about the world, publishing a story composed of miraculous accounts, and upon the strength of these accounts called upon mankind to quit the religions in which they had been educated, and to take up, thenceforth, a new system of opinions, and new rules of action. What is more in attestation of these accounts, is, that the same men voluntarily exposed themselves to harassing and perpetual labours, dangers, and sufferings. We want to know what these accounts were. We have the particulars from two of

---

* Why should not the candid and modest preface of this historian be believed, as well as that which Dion Cassius prefixes to his Life of Commodus? "These things and the following I write, not from the report of others, but from my own knowledge and observation." I see no reason to doubt but that both passages describe truly enough the situation of the authors.

their own number. We have them from an attendant of one of the number, and who was an inhabitant of Jerusalem at the time. We have them from a fourth writer, who accompanied the most laborious missionary of the institution in his travels; who was frequently brought into the society of the rest; and who begins his narrative by telling us that he is about to relate the things which had been delivered by those who were ministers of the word, and eye-witnesses of the facts. I do not know what information can be more satisfactory than this.

But I have said that if any one of the four Gospels be genuine, we have not only direct historical testimony to the point we contend for, but testimony which cannot reasonably be rejected. If the first Gospel was really written by Matthew, we have the narrative of one of the number, from which to judge what were the miracles which the apostles attributed to Jesus. Although, for argument's sake, we should allow that this Gospel had been erroneously ascribed to Matthew; yet, if the Gospel of St. John be genuine, the observation holds with no less strength. Again, although the Gospels both of Matthew and John could be spurious, yet, if the Gospel of Saint Luke were truly the composition of that person, or if the Gospel which bear the name of Mark really proceeded from him; we still, even upon the lowest supposition, possess the accounts of one writer at least, who was not only contemporary with the apostles, but associated with them in their ministry; which authority seems sufficient.

The New Testament contains a great number of distinct writings, the genuineness of any one of which is almost sufficient to prove the truth of the religion: it contains, however, four distinct histories, the genuineness of any one of which is perfectly sufficient.

Although it should appear that some of the evangelists had seen and used each other's works, this discovery, whist it subtracts indeed from their characters as testimonies strictly independent, diminishes little either their separate authority or their mutual confirmation. Let it be allowed that Mark compiled his history almost entirely from those of Matthew and Luke; and let it also for a moment be supposed that were not written by Matthew and Luke; yet, if it be true that Mark, a contemporary of the apostles, living, in habits of society with the apostles; if it be true, that this person made the compilation, it follows, that the writings from which he made it existed in the time of the apostles, and that they were then in such esteem and credit, that a companion of the apostles formed a history out of them. Let the Gospel of Mark be called an epitome of that of Matthew; if a person in the situation in which Mark is described to have been actually made the epitome, it affords the strongest possible attestation to the character of the original.

Parallelisms in sentences, in word, and in the order of words, have been traced out between the Gospel of Matthew and that of Luke; which cannot easily be explained, otherwise than by supposing, either that Luke had consulted Matthew's history, or, what appears to me in nowise incredible, that minutes of some of Christ's discourses, as well as brief memoirs of some passages of his life, had been committed to writing at the time; and that such written accounts had by both authors been occasionally admitted into their histories. Either supposition is perfectly consistent with the acknowledged formation of St. Luke's narrative, who professes to have collected them from such documents and testimonies as he judged to be authentic. Therefore, allowing that this writer also borrowed from the Gospel which we call Matthew's; yet still we have in St. Luke's Gospel a history given by a writer immediately connected with the transaction with the witnesses of it with the persons engaged in it, and composed from materials which that person deemed to be safe source of intelligence; in other words, whatever supposition be made concerning any or all the other Gospels, if Saint Luke's Gospel be genuine, we have in it a credible evidence of the point which we maintain. The Gospel according to Saint John appears to be, and is on all hands allowed to be, an independent testimony, strictly and properly so called.

Secondly: In treating of the written evidences of Christianity, we are to consider their aggregate authority. When a passage, in any wise relating to the history of Christ is read to us out of the epistle of Clemens Romanus, the epistles of Ignatius, of Polycarp, or from any other writing of that age, we are immediately sensible of the confirmation which it affords to the Scripture account. Here is a new witness. Now, if we had been accustomed to read the Gospel of Matthew alone, and had known that of Luke only as the generality of Christians know the writings of the apostolical fathers; when we came to look into what it contained, and found many of the facts which Matthew recorded, recorded also there, many other facts of a similar nature added, and throughout the whole work the same general series of transactions stated, and the same general character of the person who was the subject of the history preserved, I apprehend that we should feel our minds strongly impressed by this discovery of fresh evidence. We should feel a renewal of the same sentiment in first reading the Gospel of Saint John. That of Saint Mark perhaps would strike us as an abridgment of the history with which we were already acquainted. The very existence of four separate histories would satisfy us that the subject had a foundation; and when we observed many facts to stand the same in all; we should conclude, that they were fixed in their credit and publicity. If, after this, we should come to the knowledge of a distinct history of the same age with the rest, taking up the subject where the others had left it, and carrying on a narrative of the effects produced in the world by the extraordinary causes of which we had already been informed, we should think the reality of the original story in no little degree established by this supplement. If subsequent letters written by some of the principal agents in the business, upon the business, and during the time of their activity and concern in it, assuming all along and recognising the original story; we should find a still further support to the conclusion we had formed. The evidence does not appear to us what it is; for, being from our infancy accustomed to regard the New Testament as one book, we see in it only one testimony. Yet in this conception we are mistaken; for the very discrepancies among the several documents which form our volume prove that in their original composition they were separate, and most of them independent productions.

If we dispose our ideas in a different order, the matter stands thus:—Whilst the transaction was recent, and the original witnesses were at hand to relate it; and whilst the apostles exercised their ministry under the harassings of frequent persecutions, it is not probable that, in this engaged, anxious, and unsettled condition of life, they would think immediately of writing histories for the information of the public or of posterity.* But it is very probable, that emergencies might draw from some of them occasional letters upon the subject of their mission. Accounts in the mean time would get abroad of the extraordinary things that had been passing, with different degrees of information and correctness. The extension of the Christian society, which could no longer be instructed: by a personal intercourse with the apostles, and the possible circulation of erroneous

---

* This thought occurred to Eusebius: "Nor were the apostles of Christ greatly concerned about the writing of books, being engaged in a more excellent ministry which is above all human power." Eccles. Hist. 1. iii. c. 24.—The same consideration accounts also for the paucity of Christian writings in the first century of its aera.

narratives, would soon teach some amongst them the expediency of sending forth authentic memoirs of the life and doctrine of their Master. When accounts appeared authorised by the name, and credit, and situation of the writers, recognised by the apostles and first preachers of the religion, or found to coincide with what the apostles and first preachers of the religion had taught, other accounts would fall into; whilst these, maintaining their reputation under the test of time, inquiry, and contradiction, might be expected to make their way into the hands of Christians of all countries of the world.

This seems the natural progress of the business; and with this the records in our possession correspond. We have remaining many letters of the kind above described. But as these letters were not written to prove the truth of the Christian religion; we are not to look in them for anything more than incidental allusions to the Christian history. We are able, however, to gather from these documents attestations which have been already enumerated; and this is a species of written evidence in the highest degree satisfactory. But for our more circumstantial information, we have, in the next place, five direct histories, bearing the names of persons acquainted with the truth of what they relate, and three of them purporting, in the very body of the narrative, to be written by such persons; of which books we know, that some were in the hands of those who were contemporaries of the apostles, and that, in the age immediately posterior to that, they were received by Christians without any doubt of the truth of their accounts. In the preface to one of our histories, we have intimations left us of the existence of some ancient accounts which are now lost. It was to be expected that such accounts would swarm. When better accounts came forth, these died away. Our present histories superseded others. They soon established a reputation which does not appear to have belonged to any other.

But to return to the point which led to these reflections. By considering our records, we shall perceive that we possess a connection of proofs; and that the written evidence is of such a kind as the natural progress of things might be expected to produce.

Thirdly: The genuineness of the historical books of the New Testament is a point of importance, because the strength of their evidence is augmented by our knowledge of the situation of their authors, their relation to the subject, and the part which they sustained in the transaction; and the testimonies which we are able to produce compose a firm ground of persuasion, that the Gospels were written by the persons whose names they bear. Nevertheless, this point is not essential. The question before us is, whether the Gospels exhibit the story which the apostles and first emissaries of the religion published, and for which they acted and suffered. Now let us suppose that we possess no other information concerning these books than that they were written by early disciples of Christianity; that they were known and read during the time of the original apostles of the religion; that by Christians whom the apostles instructed, by societies of Christians which the apostles founded, these books were received, this reception would be a valid proof that these books must have accorded with what the apostles taught. A reception by the first race of Christians, is evidence that they agreed with what the first teachers of the religion delivered.

Now the fact of their early existence and reputation, is made out by some ancient testimonies which do not happen to specify the names of the writers: add to which, that two out of the four Gospels contain averments in the body of the history, which fix the time and situation of the authors. In the Gospel of St. John (xix. 35), describing the crucifixion, with the particular circumstance of piercing Christ's side with a spear, the historian adds, as for himself, "and he that saw it bare record, and his record is true, and he knoweth that he saith true, that ye might believe." Again (xxi. 24), after relating a conversation which passed between Peter and "the disciple," as it is there expressed, "whom Jesus loved," it is added, "this is the disciple which testifieth of these things, and wrote these things." This testimony is not the less worthy of regard, because it is imperfect. The name is not mentioned; which, if a fraudulent purpose had been intended, would have been done. The third of our present Gospels purports to have been written by the person who wrote the Acts of the Apostles; in which latter part of the same history, the author, by using in various places the first person plural, declares himself to have been a contemporary of all, and a companion of one, of the original preachers of the religion.

## CHAPTER IX

# OF THE AUTHENTICITY OF THE HISTORICAL SCRIPTURES, IN ELEVEN SECTIONS

We now proceed to state the distinct proofs, which show not only the general value of these records, but their specific authority, and the high probability there is that they actually came from the persons whose names they bear.

There are, however, a few preliminary reflections, by which we may draw up with more regularity to the propositions upon which the close discussion of the subject depends. Of which nature are the following:

I. We are able to produce a great number of ancient manuscripts, found in many different countries, some certainly seven or eight hundred years old, and some which have been preserved probably above a thousand years.* We have also

---

* The Alexandrian manuscript, now in the British Museum, was written probably in the fourth or fifth century.

many ancient versions of these books, and some of them into languages which are not at present, nor for many ages have been, spoken in any part of the world. The existence of these manuscripts proves that the Scriptures were not the production of any modern contrivance. The number of manuscripts, far exceeding those of any other book, and their wide dispersion, afford an argument, that the Scriptures anciently were more read than any other books, and that also in many different countries. The greatest part of spurious Christian writings are utterly lost, the rest preserved by some single manuscript. There is weight also in Dr. Bentley's observation, that the New Testament has suffered less injury by the errors of transcribers than the works of any profane author of the same size and antiquity; there never was any writing, in the preservation and purity of which the world was so careful.

II. An argument of great weight is that which arises from the style and language of the New Testament. It is just such a language as might be expected from the apostles, and from no other persons. It is the style neither of classic authors, nor of the ancient Christian fathers, but Greek coming from men of Hebrew origin; abounding with Hebraic and Syriac idioms, such as would naturally be found in the writings of men who used a language spoken where they lived, but not the common dialect of the country. This is a strong proof of the genuineness of these writings: for who should forge them? The Christian fathers were for the most part totally ignorant of Hebrew. The few who had a knowledge of the Hebrew, as Justin Martyr, Origen, and Epiphanius, wrote in a language which hears no resemblance to that of the New Testament. The Nazarenes, who understood Hebrew, used chiefly the Gospel of Saint Matthew, and therefore cannot be suspected of forging the rest of the sacred writings. The argument, at any rate, proves the antiquity of these books; that they belonged to the age of the apostles; that they could be composed in no other.*

III. Why should we question the genuineness of these books? Is it that they contain accounts of supernatural events? I apprehend that this is the real cause of our hesitation: for had the writings inscribed with the names of Matthew and John related nothing but ordinary history, there would have been no doubt at all. This reason affects the question of genuineness very indirectly. The works of Bede exhibit many wonderful relations: but who, for that reason, doubts that they were written by Bede? The same of a multitude of other authors. We ask no more for our books than what we allow to other books in some sort similar to ours.

IV. If it had been an easy thing in the early times of the institution to have forged Christian writings, and to have

---

* See this argument stated more at large in Michaelis's Introduction, (Marsh's translation,) vol. i. c. ii. sect. 10, from which these observations are taken.

obtained reception to the forgeries, we should have had many appearing in the name of Christ himself. Yet have we heard but of one attempt of this sort, so far from obtaining a reputation in anywise similar to that which can be proved to have attended the books of the New Testament, that it is not mentioned by any writer of the first three centuries. I mean the epistle of Christ to Abgarus, king of Edessa, found at present in the work of Eusebius,* after the publication of Eusebius's work, this epistle was universally rejected.[+]

V. If the ascription of the Gospels to their respective authors had been arbitrary, they would have been ascribed to more eminent men. This observation holds concerning the first three Gospels, the reputed authors of which were likely to deliver an honest account of what they knew, but were persons not distinguished in the history by extraordinary marks of notice or commendation. Of the apostles, I hardly know any one of whom less is said than of Matthew.

---

* Hist. Eccl. lib. i. c. 15.

[+] Augustin, A.D. 895 (De Consens. Evan. c. 34), had heard that the Pagans pretended to be possessed of an epistle of Christ to Peter and Paul; but he had never seen it, and appears to doubt of the existence of any such piece. No other ancient writer mentions it. The lateness of the writer who notices these things, the manner in which he notices them, and the silence of every preceding writer, render them unworthy of consideration.

Of Mark, nothing is said in the Gospels. The name of Luke is mentioned only in St Paul's epistles,* and that very transiently. The judgment, therefore, which assigned these writings to these authors proceeded, it may be presumed, upon proper evidence.

VI. Christian writers and churches appear to have soon arrived at a very general agreement upon the subject. When the diversity of opinion which prevails among Christians in other points, is considered, their concurrence in the canon of Scripture is remarkable, and of great weight, especially as it seems to have been the result of private and free inquiry. We have no knowledge of any interference of authority in the question before the council of Laodicea in the year 363. Probably the decree of this council rather declared than regulated the judgment of some neighbouring churches; the council itself consisting of no more than thirty or forty bishops of Lydia and the adjoining countries.+ Nor does its authority seem to have extended further; for we find numerous Christian writers, after this time, discussing the question, "What books were entitled to be received as Scripture," with great freedom, upon proper grounds of evidence, and without any reference to the decision at Laodicea.

---

* Col. iv. 14. 2Tim. iv. 11. Philem. 24.

+ Lardner, Cred. vol. viii. P.291, et seq.

These considerations are not to be neglected: but of an argument concerning the genuineness of ancient writings, the substance and strength, is ancient testimony.

This testimony it is necessary to exhibit somewhat in detail; for when Christian advocates merely tell us that we have the same reason for believing the Gospels to be written by the evangelists whose names they bear as we have for believing the Commentaries to be Caesar's, the Aeneid Virgil's, or the Orations Cicero's, they content themselves with an imperfect representation. The number, variety, and early date of our testimonies far exceed all other ancient books. But then it is more requisite in our books than in theirs to separate and distinguish them from spurious competitors. This circumstance renders an inquiry necessary.

In a work like the present, there is a difficulty in finding a place for evidence of this kind. To pursue the details of proof throughout, would be to transcribe a great part of Dr. Lardner's eleven octavo volumes: to leave the argument without proofs is to leave it without effect.

The method which I propose is to place before the reader, in one view, the propositions which comprise the several heads of our testimony, and afterwards to repeat the same propositions in so many distinct sections, with the necessary authorities subjoined to each.*

---

* The reader, when he has the propositions before him, will observe that the argument, if he should omit the sections, proceeds connectedly from this point.

The following, then, are the allegations upon the subject which are capable of being established by proof:—

   I. The four Gospels and the Acts of the Apostles are quoted, or alluded to, by a series of Christian writers, beginning with those who were contemporary with the apostles, or who immediately followed them, and proceeding in close and regular succession from their time to the present.

   II. That when they are quoted, or alluded to, they are quoted or alluded to with peculiar respect, as books 'sui generis'; as possessing an authority which belonged to no other books, and as conclusive in all questions and controversies amongst Christians.

   III. That they were, in very early times, collected into a distinct volume.

   IV. That they were distinguished by appropriate names and titles of respect.

   V. That they were publicly read and expounded in the religious assemblies of the early Christians.

   VI. That commentaries were written upon them, harmonies formed out of them, different copies carefully collated, and versions of them made into different languages.

VII. That they were received by Christians of
different sects, by many heretics as well,
and usually appealed to by both sides in the
controversies which arose in those days.

VIII. That the four Gospels, the Acts of the
Apostles, thirteen Epistles of Saint Paul, the
first epistle of John, and the first of Peter,
were received without doubt by those who
doubted concerning the other books which are
included in our present canon.

IX. That the Gospels were attacked by the early
adversaries of Christianity, as books containing
the accounts upon which the religion was
founded.

X. That formal catalogues of authentic Scriptures
were published; in all which our present sacred
histories were included.

XI. That these propositions cannot be affirmed
of any other books claiming to be books of
Scripture; by which are meant those books
which are commonly called apocryphal books
of the New Testament.

## SECTION I

·····················

The historical books of the New Testament are quoted, or alluded to, by a series of Christian writers, beginning with those who were contemporary with the apostles and proceeding in close and regular succession to the present.

The testimonies which we have to bring forward under this proposition are the following:—

I. There is extant an epistle ascribed to Barnabas,* the companion of Paul. It is quoted as the epistle of Barnabas, by Clement of Alexandria, A.D. CXCIV; by Origen, A.D. CCXXX. It is mentioned by Eusebius, A.D.. CCCXV, and by Jerome, A.D. CCCXCII, as an ancient work in their time, bearing the name of Barnabas, and as well known and read amongst Christians. It purports to have been written soon after the destruction of Jerusalem; and it bears the character of the age to which it professes to belong.

In this epistle appears the following remarkable passage:—"Let us, therefore, beware lest it come upon us, as it is written; There are many called, few chosen." From the expression, "as it is written," we infer that at the time when the author of this epistle lived, there was a book extant, well

---

* Lardner, Cred. edit. 1755, vol. i. p. 23, et seq. The materials of these sections are almost entirely extracted from Dr. Lardner's work; my office consisted in arrangement and selection.

known to Christians, and of authority amongst them, containing these words:—"Many are called, few chosen." Such a book is our present Gospel of Saint Matthew, in which this text is twice found, (Matt xx. 16; xxii. 14.) and is found in no other book now known.

Beside this passage, there are also in the epistle before us several others. In particular, the author of the epistle repeats the precept, "Give to every one that asketh thee;" (Matt. v. 42.) and saith that Christ chose as his apostles men who were great sinners, that he might show that he came "not to call the righteous, but sinners to repentance." (Matt. Ix. 13.)

II. We are in possession of an epistle written by Clement, bishop of Rome, (Lardner, Cred. vol. p. 62, et seq.) whom ancient writers assert to have been the Clement whom Saint Paul mentions, Phil. iv. 3; "with Clement also, and other my fellow-labourers, whose names are in the book of life." This epistle is spoken of by the ancients as acknowledged by all; and, as Irenaeus well represents its value, "written by Clement, who had seen the blessed apostles, and conversed with them; who had the preaching of the apostles still sounding in his ears, and their traditions before his eyes." It is addressed to the church of Corinth; and what alone may seem almost decisive of its authenticity, Dionysius, bishop of Corinth, about the year 170, bears witness, "that it had been wont to be read in that church from ancient times."

This epistle affords, amongst others, the following valuable passages:—"Especially remembering the words of the Lord Jesus, which he spake teaching gentleness and long-suffering: for thus he said:* Be ye merciful, that ye may obtain mercy; forgive, that it may be forgiven unto you; as you do, so shall it be done unto you; as you give, so shall it be given unto you; as ye judge, so shall ye be judged; as ye show kindness, so shall kindness be shown unto you; with what measure ye mete, with the same shall it be measured to you. By this command, and by these rules, let us establish ourselves, that we may always walk obediently to his holy words."

Again; "Remember the words of the Lord Jesus, for he said, Woe to that man by whom offences come; it were better for him that he had not been born, than that he should offend one of my elect; it were better for him that a mill-stone should be tied about his neck, and that he should be drowned in the sea, than that he should offend one of my little ones."+

---

* "Blessed are the merciful, for they shall obtain mercy." Matt. v. 7.—"Forgive, and ye shall be forgiven; give, and it shall be given unto you." Luke vi. 37, 38.—"Judge not, that ye be not judged; for with what judgment ye judge, ye shall be judged; and with what measure ye mete, it shall be measured to you again." Matt. vii. 1, 2.

+ Matt. xviii. 6. "But whoso shall offend one of these little ones which believe in me, it were better for him that a mill-stone were hanged about his neck, and that he were cast into the sea." The latter part of the passage in Clement agrees exactly with Luke xvii. 2; "It were better for him that a mill-stone were hanged about his neck, and he cast into the sea, than that he should offend one of these little ones."

In both these passages we perceive the high respect paid to the words of Christ as recorded by the evangelists; "Remember the words of the Lord Jesus;—by this command, and by these rules, let us establish ourselves, that we may always walk obediently to his holy words." We perceive also in Clement a total unconsciousness of doubt whether these were the real words of Christ, which are read as such in the Gospels. Whenever anything now read in the Gospels is met with in an early Christian writing, it is always observed to stand there as acknowledged truth. As this epistle was written in the name of the church of Rome, and addressed to the church of Corinth, it ought to be taken as exhibiting the judgment of these churches themselves.

It may be said that, as Clement has not used words of quotation, it is not certain that he refers to any book whatever. The words of Christ he might himself have heard from the apostles, or might have received through the medium of oral tradition. This has been said: but that no such inference can be drawn from the absence of words of quotation, is proved by the three following considerations:—First, that Clement, in the very same manner, uses a passage now found in the epistle to the Romans; (Rom. i. 29.) which passage, from the peculiarity of the words which compose it, and from their order, he must have taken from the book. Secondly, that there are many sentences of Saint Paul's First Epistle to the Corinthians standing in Clement's epistle without any sign of quotation, which yet certainly are quotations; because Clement had Saint Paul's epistle before him, as in one place he mentions it:—"Take into your hands the epistle of the blessed apostle Paul." Thirdly, that this method of adopting words of Scripture without reference or acknowledgment was a method in general use amongst the most ancient Christian writers.—These analogies afford a considerable degree of positive proof, that the words in question have been borrowed from the places of Scripture in which we now find them. But take it if you will the other way, that Clement had heard these words from the apostles or first teachers of Christianity; with respect to the precise point of our argument, this supposition may serve almost as well.

III. Near the conclusion of the epistle to the Romans, Saint Paul, amongst others, sends the following salutation: "Salute Asyncritus, Phlegon, Hermas, Patrobas, Hermes, and the brethren which are with them." Of Hermas, a book bearing the name is still remaining. It is called the Shepherd, (Lardner, Cred. vol. i. p. 111.) or pastor of Hermas. Its antiquity is incontestable, from the quotations of it in Irenaeus, A.D. 178; Clement of Alexandria, A.D. 194; Tertullian, A.D. 200; Origen, A.D. 230. The notes of time extant in the epistle itself agree with its title, and with the testimonies concerning it, for it purports to have been written during the life-time of Clement.

In this place are tacit allusions to Saint Matthew's, Saint Luke's, and Saint John's Gospels. In this form appear in Hermas the confessing and denying of Christ; (Matt. x.: i2, 33, or, Luke xli. 8, 9.) the parable of the seed sown (Matt. xiii. 3, or, Luke viii. 5); the comparison of Christ's disciples to little children; the saying "he that putteth away his wife, and marrieth another, committeth adultery" (Luke xvi. 18.); The singular expression, "having received all power from his Father," in probable allusion to Matt. xxviii. 18; and Christ being the "gate," or only way of coming "to God," in plain allusion to John xiv. 6; x. 7, 9. There is also a probable allusion to Acts v. 32.

It is the age in which it was composed that gives the value to its testimony.

IV. Ignatius, as it is testified by ancient Christian writers, became bishop of Antioch about thirty-seven years after Christ's ascension; and it is probable that he had known many of the apostles. Epistles of Ignatius are referred to by Polycarp, his contemporary. Passages found in the epistles now extant under his name are quoted by Irenaeus, A.D. 178; by Origen, A.D. 230; and the occasion of writing the epistles is given at large by Eusebius and Jerome. The smaller epistles of Ignatius are those which were read by Irenaeus, Origen, and Eusebius (Lardner, Cred. vol. i. p. 147.).

In these epistles are various undoubted allusions to the Gospels of Saint Matthew and Saint John; they are not accompanied with marks of quotation.

Of these allusions the following are clear specimens:

Matt.*: "Christ was baptized of John, that all righteousness might be fulfilled by him." "Be ye wise as serpents in all things, and harmless as a dove."

John[+]: "Yet the Spirit is not deceived, being from God: for it knows whence it comes and whither it goes." "He (Christ) is the door of the Father, by which enter in Abraham and Isaac, and Jacob, and the apostles, and the church."

As to the manner of quotation, this is observable;—Ignatius, in one place, speaks of St. Paul and quotes his Epistle to the Ephesians by name; yet, in several other places, he borrows words and sentiments from the same epistle without mentioning it; which shows that this was his general manner of using and applying writings then extant.

V. Polycarp (Lardner, Cred. vol. i. 192.) had been taught by the apostles and was also by the apostles appointed bishop of Smyrna.

Of Polycarp we have one undoubted epistle remaining. And this contains nearly forty clear allusions to books of the New Testament; which is strong evidence of the respect which Christians of that age bore for these books.

---

* Chap. iii. 15. "For thus it becometh us to fulfil all righteousness." Chap. x. 16. "Be ye therefore wise as serpents, and harmless as doves."

+ Chap. iii. 8. "The wind bloweth where it listeth and thou hearest the sound thereof, but canst not tell whence it cometh, and whither it goeth; so is everyone that is born of the Spirit." Chap. x. 9. "I am the door; by me if any man enter in he shall be saved."

Amongst these there are copious allusions to the Gospel of St. Matthew, some to passages found in the Gospels both of Matthew and Luke, and some which more nearly resemble the words in Luke.

I select the following as fixing the authority of the Lord's prayer, and the use of it amongst the primitive Christians: "If therefore we pray the Lord, that he will forgive us, we ought also to forgive."

"With supplication beseeching the all-seeing God not to lead us into temptation."

And the following, that words of our Lord found in our Gospels were at this early day quoted as spoken by him; and not only so, but quoted with so little question of doubt about their being really his words, as not even to mention the authority from which they were taken:

> "But remembering what the Lord said, teaching,
> Judge not, that ye be not judged; forgive, and ye shall
> be forgiven; be ye merciful, that ye may obtain mercy;
> with what measure ye mete, it shall be measured to
> you again." (Matt. vii. 1, 2; v. 7; Luke vi. 37, 38.)

Supposing Polycarp to have had these words from the books in which we now find them, it is manifest that these books were considered by him, and by his readers, as authentic accounts of Christ's discourses.

VI. Papias, (Lardner, Cred. vol. i. p. 239.) a hearer of John, and companion of Polycarp, as Irenaeus attests, in a passage quoted by Eusebius, from a work now lost, expressly ascribes the respective Gospels to Matthew and Mark; and in a manner which proves that these Gospels must have publicly borne the names of these authors at that time, and probably long before; for Papias tells us from what materials Mark collected his account, and in what language Matthew wrote. To the point for which I produce this testimony, his authority is complete.

VII. Not long after these, follows Justin Martyr (Lardner, Cred. vol. i. p. 258.). His remaining works are much larger than any that have yet been noticed. Although the nature of his two principal writings, one of which was addressed to heathens, and the other a Jew, did not lead him to such frequent appeals to Christian books; we nevertheless reckon up in them between twenty and thirty quotations of the Gospels and Acts of the Apostles, certain, distinct, and copious: if each verse be counted separately, a much greater number; if each expression, a very great one.[*]

We meet with quotations of three of the Gospels within the compass of half a page: "And in other words he says, Depart from me into outer darkness, which the Father hath prepared for Satan and his angels," (which is from Matthew xxv. 41.) "And again he said, in other words,

---

[*] "He cites our present canon, and particularly our four Gospels, continually, I dare say, above two hundred times." Jones's New and Full Method. Append. vol. i. p. 589, ed. 1726.

I give unto you power to tread upon serpents and scorpions, and venomous beasts, and upon all the power of the enemy." (This from Luke x. 19.) "And before he was crucified, he said, The Son of Man must suffer many things, and be rejected of the Scribes and Pharisees, and be crucified, and rise again the third day." (This from Mark viii. 31.)

In another place Justin quotes a passage in the history of Christ's birth, as delivered by Matthew and John, and fortifies his quotation by this remarkable testimony: "As they have taught, who have written the history of all things concerning our Saviour Jesus Christ; and we believe them." Quotations are also found from the Gospel of Saint John.

In all Justin's works, there are but two instances in which he refers to anything as said or done by Christ, which is not related concerning him in our present Gospels: which shows, that these Gospels, and these alone, were the authorities from which the Christians of that day drew the information upon which they depended. One of these instances is of a saying of Christ, not met with in any book now extant.*

The other of a circumstance in Christ's baptism, namely, a fiery or luminous appearance upon the water,

---

* "Wherefore also our Lord Jesus Christ has said, In whatsoever I shall find you, in the same I will also judge you." Possibly Justin designed not to quote any text, but to represent the sense of many of our Lord's sayings. Fabrieius has observed, that this saying has been quoted by many writers, and that Justin is the only one who ascribes it to our Lord. Words resembling these are read repeatedly in Ezekiel; "I will judge them according to their ways;" (chap. vii. 3; xxxiii. 20.) It is

which, according to Epiphanius, is noticed in the Gospel of the Hebrews, but which is mentioned by Justin, with a plain mark of diminution when compared with what he quotes as resting upon Scripture authority. The reader will advert to this distinction: "and then, when Jesus came to the river Jordan, where John was baptizing, as Jesus descended into the water, a fire also was kindled in Jordan: and when he came up out of the water, (the apostles of this our Christ have written), that the Holy Ghost lighted upon him as a dove."

All the references in Justin are made without mentioning the author; which proves that these books were perfectly notorious, and that there were no other accounts of Christ then extant as to make it necessary to distinguish these from the rest.

VIII. Hegesippus (Lardner, Cred. vol. i. p. 314.) came about thirty years after Justin. His testimony is remarkable only for this particular; that travelling from Palestine to Rome, he visited, on his journey, many bishops; and that, "in every succession, and in every city, the same doctrine is taught, which the Law and the Prophets, and the Lord teacheth."

---

remarkable that Justin had just before expressly quoted Ezekiel. Mr. Jones founded a conjecture, that Justin wrote only "the Lord hath said," intending to quote the words of God, and that some transcriber, imagining these to be the words of Christ, inserted in his copy the addition "Jesus Christ." Vol. 1. p. 539.

This is an important attestation, from good authority, and of high antiquity. It is generally understood that by the word "Lord," Hegesippus intended some writings containing the teaching of Christ; in which sense alone the term combines with the other term "Law and Prophets," which denote writings; and together with them admit of the verb "teacheth" in the present tense. Then, that these writings were some or all of the books of the New Testament, is rendered probable from hence, that in the fragments of his works, which are preserved in Eusebius, and in a writer of the ninth century, enough is left to show, that Hegesippus expressed divers thing in the style of the Gospels, and of the Acts of the Apostles; that he referred to the history in the second chapter of Matthew, and recited a text of that Gospel as spoken by our Lord.

IX. At this time, viz. about the year 170, the churches of Lyons and Vienne, in France, sent a relation of the sufferings of their martyrs to the churches of Asia and Phrygia. (Lardner, Cred. vol. i. p. 332.) The epistle is preserved entire by Eusebius. These churches had now for their bishop, Pothinus, whose early life must have joined on with the times of the apostles. In this epistle are exact references to the Gospels of Luke and John, and to the Acts of the Apostles. That from Saint John is in these words: "Then was fulfilled that which was spoken by the Lord, that whosoever killeth you, will think that he doeth God service." (John xvi. 2.)

X. Irenaeus (Lardner, vol. i. p. 344.) succeeded Pothinus as bishop of Lyons. In his youth he had been a disciple of Polycarp. In the time in which he lived, he was not much more than a century from the publication of the Gospels; in his instruction only by one step separated from the persons of the apostles. He asserts of himself and his contemporaries, that they were able to reckon up, in all the principal churches, the succession of bishops from the first. (Adv. Haeres. 1. iii. c. 3.) I remark these particulars concerning Irenaeus because the testimony which this writer affords to the historical books of the New Testament, to their authority, and to the titles which they bear, is express, positive, and exclusive. One principal passage opens with an assertion that the story which the Gospels exhibit is the story which the apostles told. "We have not received," saith Irenaeus, "the knowledge of the way of our salvation by any others than those by whom the Gospel has been brought to us. Which Gospel they first preached, and afterwards, by the will of God, committed to writing, that it might be for time to come the foundation and pillar of our faith.—For after that our Lord arose from the dead, and they (the apostles) were endowed from above with the power of the Holy Ghost coming down upon them, they received a perfect knowledge of all things. They then went forth to all the ends of the earth, declaring to men the Message of heavenly peace, having all of them, and every one, alike the Gospel of God. Matthew then, among the Jews, wrote a Gospel in their own language, while Peter and Paul were preaching the Gospel at Rome, and founding a church there: and after their exit, Mark also, the disciple and interpreter of Peter, delivered to us in writing the things that had been preached by Peter and Luke, the companion of Paul, put down in a book the Gospel preached by him (Paul). Afterwards John, the disciple of the Lord, who also leaned upon his breast, he likewise published a Gospel while he dwelt at Ephesus in Asia."

The probability that the books truly delivered what the apostles taught, is inferred also with strict regularity from another passage of his works. "The tradition of the apostles," this father saith, "hath spread itself over the whole universe; and all they who search after the sources of truth will find this tradition to be held sacred in every church, We might enumerate all those who have been appointed bishops to these churches by the apostles, and all their successors, up to our days. It is by this uninterrupted succession that we have received the tradition which actually exists in the church, as also the doctrines of truth, as it was preached by the apostles." (Iren. in Haer. I. iii. c. 3.) The reader will observe upon this, that the same Irenaeus, who is now stating the strength and uniformity of the tradition in the fullest manner, the authority of the written records; from which we are entitled to conclude, that they were then conformable to each other.

I have said that the testimony of Irenaeus in favour of our Gospels is exclusive of all others. I allude to a remarkable passage in his works, in which he endeavours to show that there could be neither more nor fewer Gospels than four. The position itself proves that only four Gospels were at that time publicly read and acknowledged. That these were our Gospels, and in the state in which we now have them, is shown from many other places beside that which we have already alleged. He mentions how Matthew begins his Gospel, how Mark begins and ends his, and their supposed reasons for so doing. He enumerates the several passages of Christ's history in Luke which are not found in any of the other evangelists. He states the particular design with which Saint John composed his Gospel, and accounts for the doctrinal declarations which precede the narrative.

To the book of the Acts of the Apostles, its author, and credit, the testimony of Irenaeus is no less explicit. Referring to the account of Saint Paul's conversion in the ninth chapter of that book, "Nor can they," says he, meaning the parties with whom he argues, "show that he is not to be credited, who has related to us the truth with the greatest exactness." In another place, he has actually collected the several texts, in which the writer is represented as accompanying Saint Paul; and delivers a summary of almost the whole of the last twelve chapters of the book.

In an author thus abounding with references and allusions to the Scriptures, there is not one to any apocryphal Christian writing whatever. This is a broad line of distinction between our sacred books and the pretensions of all others.

XI. Omitting Athenagoras and Theophilus, who lived about this time; (Lardner, vol. i. p. 400 & 422.); observing also, that the works of two learned Christian writers of the same age, Miltiades and Pantaenus, (Lardner, vol. i. p.413, 450.) are now lost, we come to one of the most voluminous of ancient Christian writers, Clement of Alexandria (Lardner, vol. ii. p. 469.). Clement followed Irenaeus at the distance of only sixteen years, and therefore may be said to maintain the series of testimony in an uninterrupted continuation.

In certain of Clement's works, now lost, but of which parts are recited by Eusebius, there is given a distinct account of the order in which the four Gospels were written. The Gospels which contain the genealogies were (he says) written first; Mark's next, at the instance of Peter's followers; and John's the last; and this account he tells us that he had received from presbyters of more ancient times. This testimony proves that these Gospels were the histories of Christ then publicly received and relied upon; and that the dates, occasions, and circumstances, of their publication were at that time subjects of inquiry amongst Christians. In the works of Clement which remain, the four Gospels are repeatedly quoted by the names of their authors, and the Acts of the Apostles is expressly ascribed to Luke. In one place he adds these remarkable words: "We have not this passage in the four Gospels delivered to us, but in that according to the Egyptians;" which puts a marked distinction between the four Gospels and all other histories of Christ. In another part, the perfect confidence with which he received the Gospels is signified: "That this is true appears from hence, that it is written in the Gospel according to Saint Luke;" and again, "I need not use many words, but only to allege the evangelic voice of the Lord." The sayings of Christ are all taken from our Gospels; the single exception to this observation appearing to be a loose quotation of a passage in Saint Matthew's Gospel.*

XII. Tertullian joins on with Clement. The number of the Gospels then received, the names of the evangelists, and their descriptions, are exhibited by this writer in one short sentence:—"Among the apostles John and Matthew teach us the faith; among apostolical men, Luke and Mark refresh it." After enumerating the churches which had been founded by Paul; by Peter and Paul, and other churches derived from John; he proceeds thus:—"I say, then, that with them, but not with them only which are apostolical, but with all who have fellowship with them in the same faith, is that Gospel of Luke received from its first publication, which we so zealously maintain:" and presently afterwards adds, "The same authority of the apostolical churches will support the other Gospels which we have from them and according to them, I mean John's and Matthew's; although that likewise

---

* "Ask great things and the small shall be added unto you." Clement chose to expound the words of Matthew (chap. vi. 33), than literally to cite them; and this is proved by another place, where he both produces the text and these words am [sic] an exposition:—Seek ye first the kingdom of heaven and its righteousness, for these are the great things; but the small things, and things relating to this life, shall be added unto you." Jones's New and Full Method, vol. i. p. 553.

which Mark published may be said to be Peter's, whose interpreter Mark was." And this evidence appears not more than one hundred and fifty years after the publication of the books.

XIII. An interval of only thirty years brings us to Origen (Lardner, vol. iii. p. 234.) of Alexandria. Nothing can be more peremptory upon the subject than the declaration of Origen, preserved by Eusebius; "That the four Gospels alone are received without dispute by the whole church of God under heaven." His attestation to the Acts of the Apostles is no less Positive: "And Luke also once more sounds the trumpet, relating the acts of the apostles." The universality with which the Scriptures were then read is well signified by this writer in a passage against Celsus, "That it is not in any private books, or such as are read by a few only, and those studious persons, but in books read by everybody, That it is written, The invisible things of God from the creation of the world are clearly seen, being understood by things that are made." It is to no purpose to single out quotations of Scripture. They are so thickly sown in the works of Origen, that Dr. Mill says, "If we had all his works remaining, we should have before us almost the whole text of the Bible." (Mill, Proleg. esp. vi. p. 66.)

XIV. The series of evidence is continued by Cyprian, bishop of Carthage, who flourished within twenty years after Origen. "The church," said this father, "is watered, like Paradise, by four rivers, that is, by four Gospels." The Acts of the Apostles is also frequently quoted by Cyprian under that name, and under the name of the "Divine Scriptures." In his various writings are such copious citations of Scripture, as to place this part of the testimony beyond controversy.

XV. Passing over a crowd* of writers following Cyprian, I single out Victorin, bishop of Pettaw, in Germany, on account of the remoteness of his situation from Origen and Cyprian, who were Africans; which proves that the Scripture histories were known and received from one side of the Christian world to the other. This bishop (Lardner, vol. v. p. 214.) lived about the year 290: and in a commentary upon this text of the Revelation, "The first was like a lion, the second was like a calf, the third like a man, and the fourth like a flying eagle," he makes out that by the four creatures are intended the four Gospels. The explication is fanciful, but the testimony positive. He also expressly cites the Acts of the Apostles.

XVI. Arnobius and Lactantius (Lardner, vol. viii. p. 43, 201.), about the year 300, composed formal arguments upon the credibility of the Christian religion. As these arguments were addressed to Gentiles, the authors abstain

---

* Novatus, Rome, A.D. 251; Dionysius, Rome, A.D. 259; Commodian, A.D. 270; Anatolius, Laodicea, A.D. 270; Theognostus A.D. 282; Methodius Lycia, A.D. 290; Phileas, Egypt, A.D. 296.

from quoting Christian books by name; but it is apparent that they draw from our Gospels, and from no other sources. Arnobius vindicates the credit of these historians. Lactantius also argues in defence of the religion, from the consistency, simplicity, disinterestedness, and sufferings of the Christian historians.

XVII. We close the series of testimonies with that of Eusebius, (Lardner, vol. viii. p. 33.) bishop of Caesarea who flourished in the year 315. This voluminous writer composed a history of the affairs of Christianity from its origin to his own time. In a passage of his Evangelical Demonstration, Eusebius remarks the delicacy of two of the evangelists, in their manner of noticing any circumstance which regarded themselves; and of Mark, as writing under Peter's direction, in the circumstances which regarded him. The illustration of this remark leads him to bring together long quotations from each of the evangelists: a proof that Eusebius, and the Christians of those days, not only read the Gospels, but studied them with attention and exactness. In a passage of his ecclesiastical History, he treats, in form, and at large, of the occasions of writing the four Gospels, and of the order in which they were written. The title of the chapter is, "Of the Order of the Gospels;" and it begins thus: "Let us observe the writings of this apostle John, which are not contradicted by any: and, first of all, must be mentioned, as acknowledged by all, the Gospel according to him, well-known to all the churches under heaven; and that it has been justly placed by the ancients the fourth in order, and after the other three, may be made evident in this manner."—Eusebius then proceeds to show that John wrote the last of the four, and that his Gospel was intended to supply the omissions of the others. He observes, "that the apostles of Christ were not studious of the ornaments of composition, nor indeed forward to write at all, being wholly occupied with their ministry."

We close this branch of our evidence here, because, after Eusebius, there is no room for any question; the works of Christian writers being as full of texts of Scripture, and of references to Scripture, as the discourses of modern divines.

## SECTION II

When the Scriptures are quoted, or alluded to, they are quoted with peculiar respect, as books sui generis; as possessing an authority which belonged to no other books, and as conclusive in all questions and controversies amongst Christians.

Beside the general strain of reference and quotation, the following may be regarded as specific testimonies:

I. Theophilus, (Lardner, Cred. part ii. vol. i. p. 429.) bishop of Antioch, the sixth in succession from the apostles, writes thus: "These things the Holy Scriptures teach us, and all who were moved by the Holy Spirit, among whom John says, In the beginning was the Word, and the Word was with God." Again: "Concerning the righteousness which the law teaches, the like things are to be found in the prophets and the Gospels, because that all, being inspired, spoke by one and the same Spirit of God." (Lardner, Cred. part ii. vol. i. p. 448.) No words can testify more strongly the high respect in which these books were holden.

II. A writer against Artemon, (Lardner, Cred. part ii. vol. iii. p. 40.) who may be supposed to come about one hundred and fifty-eight years after the publication of the Scripture, in a passage quoted by Eusebius, uses these expressions: "Possibly what they (our adversaries) say, might have been credited, if first of all the Divine Scriptures did not contradict them; and then the writings of certain brethren more ancient than the times of Victor." This passage proves, first, that there was at that time a collection called Divine Scriptures; secondly, that these Scriptures were esteemed of higher authority than the writings of the most early and celebrated Christians.

III. In a piece ascribed to Hippolytus, (Lardner, Cred. vol. iii. p. 112.) who lived near the same time, the author professes "to draw out of the sacred-fountain, and to set before him from the Sacred Scriptures what may afford him satisfaction." He then quotes immediately Paul's epistles to Timothy, and afterwards many books of the New Testament.

IV. "Our assertions and discourses," saith Origen, (Lardner, Cred. vol. iii. pp. 287–289.) "are unworthy of credit; we must receive the Scriptures as witnesses." After treating of the duty of prayer, he proceeds: "What we have said, may be proved from the Divine Scriptures." In his books against Celsus we find this passage: "That our religion teaches us to seek after wisdom, shall be shown, both out of the ancient Jewish Scriptures which we also use, and out of those written since Jesus, which are believed in the churches to be divine." These afford evidence of the exclusive authority which the Scriptures possessed.

V. Cyprian, bishop of Carthage, (Lardner, Cred. vol. vi. p. 840.) whose age lies close to that of Origen, earnestly exhorts Christian teachers "to go back to the fountain; and, if the truth has in any case been shaken, to recur to the Gospels and apostolic writings."—"The precepts of the Gospel," says he in another place, "are nothing less than authoritative divine lessons, the foundations of our hope, the supports of our faith, the guides of our way, the safeguards of our course to heaven."

VI. Novatus, (Lardner, Cred. vol. v. p. 102.) a Roman contemporary with Cyprian, appeals to the Scriptures, as the authority by which all errors were to be repelled, and disputes decided. "That Christ is not only man, but God also, is proved by the sacred authority of the Divine Writings."—"The Divine Scripture easily detects and confutes the frauds of heretics."—"It is not by the fault of the heavenly Scriptures, which never deceive."

VII. Twenty years from the writer last cited, Anatolius (Lardner, Cred. vol. v. p. 146.), bishop of Laedicea, speaking of the rule for keeping Easter, says of those whom he opposed, "They can by no means prove their point by the authority of the Divine Scripture."

VIII. The Arians, who sprung up about fifty years after this, argued against the use of the words consubstantial, essence, and like phrases; "because they were not in Scripture." (Lardner, Cred. vol. vii. pp. 283–284.) And in the same strain one of their advocates opens a conference with Augustine: "If you say what is reasonable, I must submit. If you allege anything from the Divine Scriptures which are common to both, I must hear. But unscriptural expressions (quae extra Scripturam sunt) deserve no regard."

Athanasius, the great antagonist of Arianism adds, "These are the fountain of salvation, that he who thirsts may be satisfied with the oracles contained in them. In these alone the doctrine of salvation is proclaimed. Let no man add to them, or take anything from them." (Lardner, Cred. vol. xii. p. 182.)

IX. Cyril, bishop of Jerusalem (Lardner, Cred. vol. viii. p. 276.), uses these remarkable words: "Concerning the divine and holy mysteries of faith, not the least article ought to be delivered without the Divine Scriptures." We are assured that Cyril's Scriptures were the same as ours, for he has left us a catalogue of the books included under that name.

X. Epiphanius, (Lardner, Cred. vol. viii. p. 314.) twenty years after Cyril, challenges the Arians, and the followers of Origen, "to produce any passage of the Old and New Testament favouring their sentiments."

XI. Poebadius, a Gallic bishop, who lived about thirty years after the council of Nice, testifies, that "the bishops of that council first consulted the sacred volumes, and then declared their faith." (Lardner, Cred. vol. ix. p. 52.)

XII. Basil, bishop of Caesarea, contemporary with Epiphanius, says, that "hearers instructed in the Scriptures ought to examine what is said by their teachers, and to embrace what is agreeable to the Scriptures, and to reject what is otherwise." (Lardner, Cred. vol. ix. p. 124.)

XIII. Ephraim, the Syrian, a celebrated writer of the same times, bears this conclusive testimony: "the truth written in the Sacred Volume of the Gospel is a perfect rule. Nothing can be taken from it nor added to it, without great guilt." (Lardner, Cred. vol. ix. p. 202.)

XIV. Jerome observes, concerning the quotations of Christian writers who were ancient in the year 400, that they made a distinction between books; some they quoted as of authority, and others not: which observation relates to the books of Scripture, compared with other writings, apocryphal or heathen. (Lardner, Cred. vol. x. pp. 123–124.)

## SECTION III

The Scriptures were in very early times collected into a distinct volume.

Ignatius, who was bishop of Antioch within forty years after the Ascension, and who had lived with the apostles, speaks of the Gospel and of the apostles in terms which render it very probable that he meant by the Gospel the book or volume of the Gospels, and by the apostles the book or volume of their Epistles. His words in one place are, (Lardner, Cred. part ii. vol. i. p. 180.) "Fleeing to the Gospel as the flesh of Jesus, and to the apostles as the presbytery of the church." It must be observed, that about eighty years after this we have direct proof, in the writings of Clement of Alexandria, (Lardner, Cred. part ii. vol. ii. p. 516.) that these two names, "Gospel," and "Apostles," were the names by which the writings of the New Testament, and the division of these writings, were usually expressed.

Another passage from Ignatius is:—"But the Gospel has somewhat in it more excellent, the appearance of our Lord Jesus Christ, his passion and resurrection." (Lardner, Cred. part ii. vol. ii. p. 182.)

And a third: "Ye ought to hearken to the Prophets, but especially to the gospel, in which the passion has been manifested to us, and the resurrection perfected." In this last passage, the Prophets and the Gospel are put in conjunction; and as Ignatius undoubtedly meant by the prophets a collection of writings, it is probable that he meant the same by the Gospel.

This interpretation of the word "Gospel," quoted from Ignatius, is confirmed by the relation of the martyrdom of Polycarp by the church of Smyrna. "All things," say they, "that went before, were done, that the Lord might show us a martyrdom according to the Gospel, for he expected to be delivered up as the Lord also did." (Ignat. Ep. c.i.) And in another place, "We do not commend those who offer themselves, forasmuch as the Gospel, teaches us no such thing." (Ignat. Ep. c. iv.) In both these places, what is called the Gospel seems to be the history of Jesus Christ, and of his doctrine.

II. Eusebius relates, that the immediate successors of the apostles, travelling abroad, carried the Gospels with them, and delivered them to their converts. The words of Eusebius are: "Then travelling abroad, they performed the work of evangelists, being ambitious to preach Christ, and deliver the Scripture of the divine Gospels." (Lardner, Cred. part ii. vol. i. p. 236.) Eusebius had before him the writings of many of that age, which are now lost.

III. Irenaeus, in the year 178, (Lardner, Cred. part ii. vol. i. p. 383.) puts the evangelic and apostolic writings in connexion with the Law and the Prophets, manifestly intending by the one a code or collection of Christian sacred writings, as the other expressed the code or collection of Jewish sacred writings.

IV. Melito, at this time bishop of Sardis, writing to one Onesimus, tells his correspondent, (Lardner, Cred. vol. i. p. 331.) that he had procured an accurate account of the books of the Old Testament. The term Old Testament certainly does prove that there was then a volume or collection of writings called the New Testament.

V. In the time of Clement of Alexandria it is apparent that the Christian Scriptures were divided into two parts, under the general titles of the Gospels and Apostles; and that both these were regarded as of the highest authority. One out of many expressions of Clement, alluding to this distribution, is: "There is a consent and harmony between the Law and the Prophets, the Apostles and the Gospel." (Lardner, Cred. vol. ii. p. 516.)

VI. The same division, "Prophets, Gospels, and Apostles," appears in Tertullian, the contemporary of Clement. The collection of the Gospels is likewise called by this writer the "Evangelic Instrument;" the whole volume the "New Testament;" and the two parts, the "Gospels and Apostles." (Lardner, Cred. vol. ii. pp. 631, 574 & 632.)

VII. From many writers also of the third century, it is collected that the Christian Scriptures were divided into two volumes, one called the "Gospels or Scriptures of the Lord," the other the "Apostles, or Epistles of the Apostles" (Lardner, Cred. vol. iv. p. 846.)

VIII. Eusebius takes some pains to show that the Gospel of Saint John had been justly placed by the ancients, "the fourth in order, and after the other three." (Lardner, Cred. vol. viii. p. 90.) The very introduction of such an argument proves that the four Gospels had been collected into a volume; that their order had been adjusted with much consideration, and that this had been done by those who were called ancients in the time of Eusebius.

In the Diocletian persecution, in the year 303, the Scriptures were sought out and burnt: (Lardner, Cred. vol. vii. pp. 214 et seq.) many suffered death rather than deliver them up. On the other hand, Constantine, after his conversion, gave directions for multiplying copies of the Divine Oracles, and for magnificently adorning them. (Lardner, Cred. vol. vii. p. 432.) What the Christians of that age so richly embellished and so tenaciously preserved under persecution, was the very volume of the New Testament which we now read.

## SECTION IV

Our present Sacred Writings were soon distinguished by appropriate names and titles of respect.

Polycarp. "I trust that ye are well exercised in the Holy Scriptures;—as in these Scriptures it is said, Be ye angry and sin not, and let not the sun go down upon your wrath." (Lardner, Cred. vol. i. p. 203.) This passage proves that, in the time of Polycarp, there were Christian writings distinguished by the name of "Holy Scriptures," or Sacred Writings. Moreover, the text quoted is a text found in the collection at this day. (Lardner, Cred. vol. i. p. 223.) In another place, Polycarp has these words: "Whoever perverts the Oracles of the Lord to his own lusts, and says there is neither resurrection nor judgment, he is the first born of Satan." (Lardner, Cred. vol. i. p. 223.)—It does not appear what else Polycarp could mean by the "Oracles of the Lord," but those same "Holy Scriptures," of which he had spoken before.

II. Justin Martyr, about thirty years after Polycarp's epistle, expressly cites some of our present histories under the title of Gospel. His words are these:—"For the apostles in the memoirs composed by them, which are called Gospels, have thus delivered it, that Jesus commanded them to take bread, and give thanks." (Lardner, Cred. vol. i. p. 271.) There exists no doubt, but that, by the memoirs abovementioned, Justin meant our present historical Scriptures; for he quotes these and no others.

III. Dionysius, bishop of Corinth, who came thirty years after Justin, in a passage preserved in Eusebius, speaks "of the Scriptures of the Lord." (Lardner, Cred. vol. i. p. 298.)

IV. And at the same time, by Irenaeus, bishop of Lyons in France, they are called "Divine Scriptures,"—"Divine Oracles,"—"Scriptures of the Lord,"—"Evangelic and Apostolic writings." (Lardner, Cred. vol. i. p. 343, et seq.)

The quotations of Irenaeus prove decidedly, that our present Gospels, and these alone, together with the Acts of the Apostles, were the historical books comprehended by him under these appellations.

V. Saint Matthew's Gospel is quoted by Theophilus, bishop of Antioch, under the title of the "Evangelic voice;" (Lardner, Cred. vol. i. p. 427.) and the copious works of Clement of Alexandria, within fifteen years of the same time, ascribe to the books of the New Testament the various titles of "Sacred Books,"—"Divine Scriptures,"—"Divinely inspired Scriptures,"—"Scriptures of the Lord,"—"the true Evangelical Canon." (Lardner, Cred. vol. ii. p. 515.)

VI. Tertullian, beside adopting most of the names and epithets above noticed, calls the Gospels "our Digesta," in allusion to some collection of Roman laws then extant. (Lardner, Cred. vol. ii. p. 630.)

VII. By Origen, who came thirty years after Tertullian, the same titles are applied to the Christian Scriptures: and, in addition thereunto, this writer frequently speaks of the "Old and New Testament,"—"the Ancient and New Scriptures,"—"the Ancient and New Oracles." (Lardner, Cred. vol. iii. p. 230.)

VIII. In Cyprian, who was not twenty years later, they are "Books of the Spirit,"—"Divine Fountains,"—"Fountains of the Divine Fulness." (Lardner, Cred. vol. iv. p. 844.)

The expressions we have thus quoted are evidences of high and peculiar respect. They all occur within two centuries from the publication of the books.

## SECTION V

Our Scriptures were publicly read and expounded in the religious assemblies of the early Christians. Justin Martyr, who wrote in the year 140, has this remarkable passage:

"The Memoirs of the Apostles, or the Writings of the Prophets, are read according as the time allows: and, when the reader has ended, the president makes a discourse, exhorting to the imitation of so excellent things." (Lardner, Cred. vol. i. p. 273.)

A few short observations will show the value of this testimony.

1. The "Memoirs of the Apostles," Justin in another place expressly tells us, are what are called "Gospels:" and that they were the Gospels which we now use, is made certain by Justin's numerous quotations of them.

2. Justin describes the general usage of the Christian church.

3. Justin does not speak of it as newly instituted, but in the terms of established customs.

II. Tertullian, who followed Justin at the distance of about fifty years, in his account of the religious assemblies of Christians, says, "We come together to recollect the Divine Scriptures; we nourish our faith, raise our hope, confirm our trust, by the Sacred Word." (Lardner, Cred. vol. ii. p. 628.)

III. Eusebius records of Origen, that when he went into Palestine about the year 216, he was desired by the bishops of that country to discourse and expound the Scriptures publicly in the church. (Lardner, Cred. vol. iii. p. 68.) This anecdote recognises the usage, not only of reading, but of expounding the Scriptures. Origen also himself bears witness to the same practice: "This," says he, "we do, when the Scriptures are read in the church, and when the discourse for explication is delivered to the people." (Lardner, Cred. vol. iii. p. 302.) And many homilies of his upon the Scriptures of the New Testament are still extant.

IV. Cyprian, whose age was not twenty years lower than that of Origen, gives an account of having ordained two persons, who were before confessors, to be readers; and what they were to read appears by the reason which he gives for his choice; "Nothing," says Cyprian, "can be more fit than that he who has made a glorious confession of the Lord should read publicly in the church; that he who has shown himself willing to die a martyr should read the Gospel of Christ by which martyrs are made." (Lardner, Cred. vol. iv. p. 842.)

V. Intimations of the same custom may be traced throughout the whole of the fourth century. Augustine, near the conclusion of the century, displays the benefit of the public reading of the Scriptures in the churches, "where," says he, "is a consequence of all sorts of people of both sexes; and where they hear how they ought to live well in this world, that they may deserve to live happily and eternally in another." And this custom he declares to be universal: "The canonical books of Scripture being read every where, the miracles therein recorded are well known to all people." (Lardner, Cred. vol. x. p. 276, et seq.)

There is not the least evidence, that any other Gospel than the four which we receive was ever admitted to this distinction.

## SECTION VI

Commentaries were anciently written upon the Scriptures; harmonies formed out of them; different copies carefully collated; and versions made of them into different languages.

No greater proof can be given of the esteem in which these books were holden by the ancient Christians, than the industry bestowed upon them. And the importance of these books consisted in their genuineness and truth. Moreover, it shows that they were even then considered as ancient books. Men do not write comments upon publications of their own times.

I. Tatian, who flourished about the year 170, composed a harmony, or collation of the Gospels, which he called Diatessaron. The title, as well as the work, shows that then, as now, there were only four Gospels in general use with Christians. (Lardner, Cred. vol. i. p. 307.)

II. Pantaenus, who came twenty years after Tatian, wrote many commentaries upon the Holy Scriptures, which, as Jerome testifies, were extant in his time. (Lardner, Cred. vol. i. p. 455.)

III. Clement of Alexandria wrote short explications of many books of the Old and New Testament. (Lardner, Cred. vol. ii. p. 462.)

IV. Tertullian appeals from the authority of a later version, then in use, to the authentic Greek. (Lardner, Cred. vol. ii. p. 638.)

V. An anonymous author, quoted by Eusebius, and who appears to have written about the year 212, appeals to the ancient copies of the Scriptures, in refutation of some corrupt readings. (Lardner, Cred. vol. iii. p. 46.)

VI. The same Eusebius, mentioning by name several writers of the church, and concerning whom he says, "There still remain divers monuments of the laudable industry of those ancient and ecclesiastical men," adds, "There are, besides, treatises of many others, whose names we have not been able to learn, orthodox and ecclesiastical men, as the interpretations of the Divine Scriptures given by each of them show." (Lardner, Cred. vol. ii. p. 551.)

VII. The last five testimonies may be referred to the year 200; immediately after which, a period of thirty years gives us Julius Africanus, who wrote an epistle upon the difference in the genealogies in Matthew and Luke, which he endeavours to reconcile by the distinction of natural and legal descent. (Lardner, Cred. vol. iii. p. 170.)

Ammonius, a learned Alexandrian, who composed a harmony of the four Gospels, which proves, as Tatian's did, that there were four Gospels at this time. It affords also on instance of the zeal of Christians for those writings. (Lardner, Cred. vol. iii. p. 122.)

And, above both these, Origen, who wrote commentaries upon most of the books included in the New Testament (Lardner, Cred. vol. iii. pp. 352, 192, 202 & 245.)

VIII. In addition to these, the third century likewise contains—Dionysius of Alexandria, who compared, with great accuracy, the accounts in the four Gospels of the time of Christ's resurrection, adding a reflection which showed his opinion of their authority: "Let us not think that the evangelists disagree or contradict each other, although there be some small difference; but let us honestly and faithfully endeavour to reconcile what we read." (Lardner, Cred. vol. iv. p. 166.)

Victorin, bishop of Pettaw, in Germany, who wrote comments upon Saint Matthew's Gospel. (Lardner, Cred. vol. iv. p. 195.)

Lucian, a presbyter of Antioch; and Hesychius, an Egyptian bishop, who put forth editions of the New Testament.

IX. The fourth century supplies a catalogue* of fourteen writers whose works or names are come down to our times; amongst which it may be sufficient to notice the following:

Eusebius wrote expressly upon the discrepancies observable in the Gospels, and a treatise, in which he pointed out what things are related by four, what by three, what by two, and what by one evangelist. (Lardner, Cred. vol. viii. p. 46.) This author also testifies what is a material piece of evidence, "that the writings of the apostles had obtained such an esteem as to be translated into every language both of Greeks and Barbarians, and to be diligently studied by all nations." (Lardner, Cred. vol. viii. p. 201.) This testimony was given about the year 300.

---

* Eusebius ..... A.D. 315
  Juvencus, Spain ..... 330
  Theodore, Thrace ..... 334
  Hilary, Poletiers ..... 340
  Fortunatus ..... 354
  Apollinarius of Loadicea ..... 362
  Damasus, Rome ..... 366

  Gregory, Nyssen ..... 371
  Didimus of Alex, ..... 370
  Ambrose of Milan ..... 374
  Diodore of Tarsus ..... 378
  Gaudent of Brescia ..... 387
  Theodore of Cilicia ..... 395
  Jerome ..... 392
  Chrysostom ...... 398

Damasus, bishop of Rome, in a letter still remaining, desires Jerome to give him a clear explanation of the word Hosanna, found in the New Testament; "He (Damasus) having met with very different interpretations of it in the Greek and Latin commentaries of Catholic writers which he had read." (Lardner, Cred. vol. ix. p. 108) This last clause shows the number and variety of commentaries then extant.

Gregory of Nyssen, at one time, appeals to the most exact copies of Saint Mark's Gospel; at another time, compares, and proposes to reconcile, the several accounts of the Resurrection given by the four Evangelists; which limitation proves that there were no other histories of Christ deemed authentic beside these. This writer observes, that "the disposition of the clothes in the sepulchre, the napkin that was about our Saviour's head, not lying with the linen clothes, but wrapped together in a place by itself, did not bespeak the terror and hurry of thieves, and therefore refutes the story of the body being stolen." (Lardner, Cred. vol. ix. p. 163.)

Ambrose, bishop of Milan, remarked various readings in the Latin copies of the New Testament, and appeals to the original Greek;

And Jerome put forth an edition of the New Testament in Latin, corrected, at least as to the Gospels, by Greek copies, and "those (he says) ancient."

Lastly, Chrysostom published a great many sermons upon the Gospels and the Acts of the Apostles.

There is no example of Christian writers of the first three centuries composing comments upon any other books than those which are found in the New Testament, except the single one of Clement of Alexandria commenting upon a book called the Revelation of Peter.

Of the ancient versions of the New Testament, one of the most valuable is the Syriac. Syriac was the language of Palestine when Christianity was there first established. And although the books of Scripture were written in Greek, it is probable that they would soon be translated into the language of the country. Accordingly, a Syriac translation is now extant, bearing many internal marks of high antiquity, confirmed by the discovery of many very ancient manuscripts in the libraries of Europe, It is about 200 years since a bishop of Antioch sent a copy of this translation into Europe; and this seems to be the first time that the translation became generally known. The bishop of Antioch's Testament was found to contain all our books, except the second epistle of Peter, the second and third of John, and the Revelation; which books have since been discovered in that language in some ancient manuscripts of Europe. And the text, though preserved in a remote country, and without communication with ours, differs from ours very little, and in nothing that is important (Jones on the Canon, vol. i. e. 14.).

## SECTION VII

Our Scriptures were received by ancient Christians of different sects and were usually appealed to by both sides in the controversies which arose in those days.

The three most ancient topics of controversy amongst Christians were, the authority of the Jewish constitution, the origin of evil, and the nature of Christ. Upon the first we find, in very early times, one class of heretics rejecting the Old Testament entirely; another contending for the obligation of its law over every one who sought acceptance with God. Upon the two latter subjects, a natural curiosity, prompted by the scholastic habits of the age, which carried men much into bold hypotheses, raised, amongst some who professed Christianity, very wild and unfounded opinions. It is a great satisfaction to perceive what, in a vast plurality of instances, we do perceive, all sides recurring to the same Scriptures.

*I. Basilides lived about the year 120. (Lardner, vol. ix. p. 271.) He rejected the Jewish institution as proceeding from a being inferior to the true God; and advanced a theology widely different from the general doctrine of the Christian church. There is positive evidence that Basilides received the Gospel of Matthew; and there is no sufficient proof that he rejected any of the other three: on the contrary, it appears that he wrote a commentary upon the Gospel. (Lardner, vol. ix. ed. 1788, p. 305, 306.)

-----

* The materials of the former part of this section are taken from Dr. Lardner's History of the Heretics of the first two centuries, published since his death, with additions, by the Rev. Mr. Hogg, of Exeter, and inserted into the ninth volume of his works, of the edition of 1778.

II. The Valentinians appeared about the same time. Their heresy consisted in notions concerning angelic natures. Of this sect, Irenaeus, who wrote A.D. 172, expressly records that they endeavoured to fetch arguments for their opinions from the evangelic and apostolic writings. Heracleon, one of the most celebrated of the sect, wrote commentaries upon Luke and John. Some observations of his upon Matthew are preserved by Origen. Nor is there any reason to doubt that he received the whole New Testament. (Lardner, vol. ix. ed. 1788, pp. 350-351; vol. i. p. 383; vol. ix. ed. 1788, p. 352–353.)

III. The Carpocratians were also an early heresy. Some of their opinions resembled Socinianism. They are specifically charged, by Irenaeus and Epiphanius, with endeavouring to pervert a passage in Matthew, which amounts to a positive proof that they received that Gospel. (Lardner, vol. ix. ed. 1788, pp. 309 & 318.)

IV. The Sethians, A.D. 150; the Montanists, A.D. 156; the Marcosigns, A.D. 160; Hermogenes, A.D. 180; Praxias, A.D. 196; Artemon, A.D. 200; Theodotus, A.D. 200; all included under the denomination of heretics, received the Scriptures of the New Testament. (Lardner, vol. ix. ed. 1788, pp. 455, 482, 348, 473, 433, 466.)

V. Tatian, who lived in the year 172, was the founder of a sect called Encratites, and was deeply involved in disputes with the Christians of that age; yet Tatian so received the four Gospels as to compose a harmony from them.

VI. From a writer quoted by Eusebius, of about the year 200, it is apparent that they who at that time contended for the mere humanity of Christ, argued from the Scriptures; for they are accused of making alterations in their copies in order to favour their opinions. (Lardner, vol. iii. P. 46.)

VII. Origen's sentiments excited great controversies,— the bishops of Rome and Alexandria condemning, the bishops of the east espousing them; yet both the advocates and adversaries of these opinions acknowledged the same authority of Scripture. In his time many dissensions subsisted amongst Christians, with which they were reproached by Celsus; yet Origen, who has recorded this accusation without contradicting it, nevertheless testifies, that the four Gospels were received without dispute, by the whole church of God. (Lardner, vol. iv. ed. 1788, p. 642.)

VIII. Paul of Samosata, about thirty years after Origen, so distinguished himself in the controversy concerning the nature of Christ as to be the subject of two councils. Yet he is not charged by his adversaries with rejecting any book of the New Testament. On the contrary, Epiphanius, who wrote a history of heretics a hundred years afterwards, says, that Paul endeavoured to support his doctrine by texts of Scripture. And Vincentius Lirinensis, A.D. 434, speaking of

Paul and other heretics of the same age, has these words: "Here, perhaps, some one may ask whether heretics also urge the testimony of Scripture. They urge it, indeed, explicitly and vehemently; for you may see them flying through every book of the sacred law." (Lardner, vol. ix. p. 158.)

IX. A controversy at the same time existed with the Noetians or Sabellians, who seem to have gone into the opposite extreme from that of Paul of Samosata. Yet according to the express testimony of Epiphanius, Sabellius received all the Scriptures. And with both sects Catholic writers constantly allege the Scriptures, and reply to the arguments which their opponents drew from particular texts.

We have here, therefore, a proof, that parties who were the most irreconcilable to one another acknowledged the authority of Scripture with equal deference.

X. And as a general testimony to the same point, may be produced what was said by one of the bishops of the council of Carthage:—"I am of opinion that blasphemous and wicked heretics, who pervert the sacred and adorable words of the Scripture, should be execrated." Undoubtedly, what they perverted they received. (Lardner, vol. ix. p. 839.)

XI. The Millennium, Novatianism, the baptism of heretics, the keeping of Easter, engaged also the attention and divided the opinions of Christians, at and before that time; yet every one appealed for the grounds of his opinion to Scripture authority. Dionysius of Alexandria, who flourished A.D. 247, describing a public disputation, with the Millennarians of Egypt, confesses of them, "that they embrace whatever could be made out by good arguments, from the Holy Scriptures." (Lardner, vol. iv. p. 666.) Novatus, A.D. 251, the founder of a numerous sect, quotes the Gospel with the same respect as other Christians did; and concerning his followers, the testimony of Socrates, who wrote about the year 440, is positive, viz. "That in the disputes between the Catholics and them, each side endeavoured to support itself by the authority of the Divine Scriptures" (Lardner, vol. v. p. 105.)

XII. The Donatists, in the year 328, used the same Scriptures as we do. "Produce," saith Augustine, "some proof from the Scriptures, whose authority is common to us both" (Lardner, vol. vii. p. 243.)

XIII. It is notorious, that in the Arian controversy, which arose soon after the year 300, both sides appealed to the same Scriptures. The Arians, in their council of Antioch, A.D. 341, pronounce that "if any one, contrary to the sound doctrine of the Scriptures, say, that the Son is a creature, as one of the creatures, let him be an anathema." (Lardner, vol. vii. p. 277.) They and the Athanasians mutually accuse each other of using unscriptural phrases; which was a mutual acknowledgment of the conclusive authority of Scripture.

XIV. The Priscillianists, A.D. 378, the Pelagians, A.D. 405 received the same Scriptures as we do. (Lardner, vol. ix. p. 325; vol. xi p. 52.)

XV. The testimony of Chrysostom, who lived near the year 400, may form a proper conclusion of the argument. "The general reception of the Gospels is a proof that their history is true and consistent; for, since the writing of the Gospels, many heresies have arisen, holding opinions contrary to what is contained in them, who yet receive the Gospels either entire or in part." (Lardner, vol. x. p. 316.) I am not moved by, "entire or in part;" for if all the parts which were ever questioned in our Gospels were given up, it would not affect the miraculous origin of the religion in the smallest degree.

Of all the ancient heretics, the most extraordinary was Marcion. (Lardner, vol. ix. sect. ii. c. x. Also Michael vol. i. c. i. sect. xviii.) One of his tenets was the rejection of the Old Testament, as proceeding from an inferior and imperfect Deity; and he erased from the New every passage which recognised the Jewish Scriptures. Yet this rash and wild controversialist published a chastised edition of Saint Luke's Gospel, containing the leading facts, and all which is necessary to authenticate the religion. This example affords proof that there were always the main points, which neither the fury of opposition nor the intemperance of controversy, would venture to call in question. There is no reason to believe that Marcion, though full of resentment against the Catholic Christians, ever charged them with forging their books. "The Gospel of Saint Matthew, the Epistle to the Hebrews, with those of Saint Peter and Saint James, as well as the Old Testament in general" he said, "were writings not for Christians but for Jews." This declaration shows the ground upon which Marcion proceeded in his mutilation of the Scriptures. Marcion flourished about the year 130.*

Dr. Lardner, in his General Review, sums up this head of evidence in the following words:—"Noitus, Paul of Samosata, Sabellius, Marcelins, Photinus, the Novatiana, Donatists, Manicheans (This must be with an exception, however, of Faustus, who lived so late as the year 354), Priscillianists, beside Artemon, the Audians, the Arians, and divers others, all received most of all the same books of the New Testament which the Catholics received; and agreed in a like respect for them as written by apostles, or their disciples and companions." (Lardner, vol. iii. p. 12.)

## SECTION VIII

The four Gospels, the Acts of the Apostles, thirteen Epistles of Saint Paul, the First Epistle of John, and the First of Peter, were received without doubt by those who doubted concerning the other books which are included in our present Canon.

---

* I have transcribed this sentence from Michaelis (p. 38), who has not, however, referred to the authority upon which he attributes these words to Marcion.

I state this proposition, because it shows that the authenticity of their books was a subject amongst the early Christians of consideration and inquiry; and that, where there was cause of doubt, they did doubt; which strengthens their testimony to such books as were received by them with full acquiescence.

I. Jerome, in his account of Caius, who flourished near the year 200, records that, reckoning up only thirteen epistles of Paul, he says the fourteenth, which is inscribed to the Hebrews, is not his: and then Jerome adds, "With the Romans to this day it is not looked upon as Paul's." This agrees with the account given by Eusebius of the same ancient author and his work; except that Eusebius delivers his own remark in more guarded terms: "And indeed to this very time, by some of the Romans, this epistle is not thought to be the apostle's." (Lardner, vol. iii. p. 240.)

II. Origen, about twenty years after Caius, quoting the Epistle to the Hebrews, observes that some might dispute the authority of that epistle; and therefore proceeds to quote as undoubted books of Scripture, the Gospel of Saint Matthew, the Acts of the Apostles, and Paul's First Epistle to the Thessalonians. (Lardner, vol. iii. p. 246.) And in another place, this author speaks of the Epistle to the Hebrews thus: "The account come down to us is various; some saying that Clement who was bishop of Rome, wrote this epistle; others, that it was Luke, the same who wrote the Gospel and the Acts." Speaking also, in the same paragraph, of Peter, "Peter," says he, "has left one epistle, acknowledged; let it be granted likewise that he wrote a second, for it is doubted of." And of John, "He has also left one epistle, of a very few lines; grant also a second and a third, for all do not allow them to be genuine." Now let it be noted, that Origen, who thus confesses his own doubts and the doubts which subsisted in his time, expressly witnesses concerning the four Gospels, "that they alone are received without dispute by the whole church of God under heaven." (Lardner, vol. iii. p. 234.)

III. Dionysius of Alexandria, in the year 247, doubts whether the Book of Revelation was written by Saint John; states his doubt, represents the diversity of opinion concerning it, in his own time, and before his time. (Lardner, vol. iv. p. 670.) Yet the same Dionysius uses and collates the four Gospels in a manner which shows that they, and they alone, were received as authentic histories of Christ. (Lardner, vol. iv. p. 661.)

IV. But this section may be said to have been framed to introduce two remarkable passages extant in Eusebius's Ecclesiastical History. The first opens:—"Let us observe the writings of the apostle John which are uncontradicted: and first of all must be mentioned, as acknowledged of all, the Gospel according to him, well known to all the churches under heaven." The author then proceeds to relate the occasions of writing the Gospels, and the reasons for placing Saint John's the last, manifestly speaking of all the four as parallel in their authority, and in the certainty of their original. (Lardner, vol. viii. p. 90.) The second passage is taken from a chapter, the title of which is, "Of the Scriptures universally acknowledged, and of those that are not such." Eusebius begins his enumeration: "In the first place are to be ranked the sacred four Gospels; then the book of the Acts of the Apostles; after that are to be reckoned the Epistles of Paul. In the next place, that called the First Epistle of John, and the Epistle of Peter, are to be esteemed authentic. After this is to be placed, if it be thought fit, the Revelation of John, about which we shall observe the different opinions at proper seasons. Of the controverted, but yet well known or approved by the most, are, that called the Epistle of James, and that of Jude, and the Second of Peter, and the Second and Third of John, whether they are written by the evangelist, or another of the same name." (Lardner, vol. viii. p. 39.) He then proceeds to reckon up five others, not in our canon, which he calls controverted.

It is manifest from this passage, that the four Gospels, and the Acts of the Apostles, were acknowledged without dispute, even by those who raised objections about some other parts of the same collection. The author was extremely conversant in the writings of Christians which had been published from the commencement of the institution to his own time: and it was from these writings that he drew his knowledge of the character and reception of the books in question. Eusebius recurred to this medium of information: "None," he says, "of the ecclesiastical writers, in the succession of the apostles, have vouchsafed to make any mention of them in their writings;" and, by another passage of the same work, wherein, speaking of the First Epistle of Peter, "This," he says, "the presbyters of ancient times have quoted in their writings as undoubtedly genuine;" (Lardner, vol. viii. p. 99.) and then, speaking of some other writings bearing the name of Peter, "We know," he says, "that they have not been delivered down to us in the number of Catholic writings, forasmuch as no ecclesiastical writer of the ancients, or of our times, has made use of testimonies out of them." "But in the progress of this history," the author proceeds, "we shall make it our business to show, together with the successions from the apostles, what ecclesiastical writers, in every age, have used such writings as these which are contradicted, and what they have said with regard to the Scriptures received in the New Testament, and acknowledged by all, and with regard to those which are not such." (Lardner, vol. viii. p. 111)

After this it is reasonable to believe that when Eusebius states the four Gospels, and the Acts of the Apostles, as uncontradicted, uncontested, and acknowledged by all; and when he places them in opposition, not only to those which were spurious, but to those which were controverted, and even to those which were well known and approved by many, yet doubted of by some; he represents not only the sense of his own age, but the result of the evidence which the writings of prior ages had furnished. The opinion of Eusebius and his contemporaries appears to have been founded upon the testimony of writers whom they then called ancient: and such of the works of these writers as have come down to our times entirely confirm the judgment. The books which he calls "books universally acknowledged" are in fact used and quoted in remaining works of Christian writers, during the 250 years between the apostles' time and that of Eusebius, much more frequently than, and in a different manner from, those the authority of which was disputed.

## SECTION IX

Our historical Scriptures were attacked by the early adversaries of Christianity, as containing the accounts upon which the Religion was founded.

Near the middle of the second century, Celsus, a heathen philosopher, wrote a professed treatise against Christianity. Origen, who came about fifty years after him, published an answer, in which he frequently recites his adversary's words and arguments. The work of Celsus is lost; but that of Origen remains. Origen appears to have given us the words of Celsus very faithfully; and amongst other reasons for thinking so, this is one, that the objection is sometimes stronger than his own answer:

"That it may not be suspected," Celsus says, "that we pass by any chapters because we have no answers at hand,

I have thought it best, according to my ability, to confute everything proposed by him, not so much observing the natural order of things, as the order which he has taken himself." (Orig. cont. Cels. I. i. sect. 41.)

Celsus wrote about one hundred years after the Gospels were published. The reception, credit, and notoriety of these books must have been well established amongst Christians, to have made them subjects of opposition by strangers and by enemies. It evinces the truth of what Chrysostom, two centuries afterwards, observed, that "the Gospels, when written, were not hidden in a corner or buried in obscurity, but they were made known to all the world, before enemies as well as others, even as they are now." (In Matt. Hom. I. 7.)

1. Celsus uses these words:—"I could say many things concerning the affairs of Jesus, and those, too, different from those written by the disciples of Jesus; but I purposely omit them." (Lardner, Jewish and Heathen Test. vol. ii. p. 274.) It is not easy to believe, that if Celsus could have contradicted the disciples upon good evidence, he would have omitted to do so.

   It is sufficient, however, to prove that, in the time of Celsus, there were books well known, and allowed to be written by the disciples of Jesus, which books contained a history of him.

2. In another passage, Celsus accuses the Christians of altering the Gospel. (Lardner, Jewish and

Heathen Test. Vol. ii. p. 275.) The accusation
refers to variations in the readings of particular
passages. We cannot perceive that Celsus
specified any particular instances, and without
such specification the charge is of no value. But
the true conclusion to be drawn from it is, that
there were in the hands of the Christian histories
which were even then of some standing: for
various readings and corruptions do not take
place in recent productions.

3.  In a third passage, the Jew whom Celsus
    introduces shuts up an argument:—"these
    things then we have alleged to you out of your
    own writings, not needing any other weapons."
    (Lardner, vol. ii. p. 276.) It is manifest that this
    boast proceeds upon the supposition that the
    books over which the writer affects to triumph
    possessed an authority by which Christians
    confessed themselves to be bound.

4.  That the books to which Celsus refers were no
    other than our present Gospels, is made out by
    his allusions to various passages still found in
    these Gospels.

Celsus not only perpetually referred to the accounts of
Christ contained in the four Gospels, but he founded none
of his objections to Christianity upon any thing delivered
in spurious Gospels.

II. What Celsus was in the second century, Porphyry became in the third. His large and formal treatise against the Christian religion is not extant. We must gather his objections from Christian writers, who have noticed in order to answer them; and enough remains to prove completely, that Porphyry's animadversions were directed against the contents of our present Gospels, and of the Acts of the Apostles; Porphyry considering that to overthrow them was to overthrow the religion.

Porphyry had read the Gospels with that sort of attention which a writer would employ who regarded them as the depositaries of the religion which he attacked. There exists general evidence that the places of Scripture upon which Porphyry had remarked were very numerous.

What was said of Celsus is true likewise of Porphyry, that it does not appear that he considered any history of Christ except these as having authority with Christians.

III. A third great writer against the Christian religion was the emperor Julian, whose work was composed about a century after that of Porphyry.

In various long extracts, transcribed from this work by Cyril and Jerome, it appears, (Jewish and Heathen Test. vol. iv. p. 77, et seq.) that Julian noticed by name Matthew and Luke, in the difference between their genealogies of Christ that he objected to Matthew's application of the prophecy, "Out of Egypt have I called my son" (ii. 15), and to that of "A virgin shall conceive" (i. 23); that he recited sayings of Christ, and various passages of his history, in the very words of the evangelists; that he alleged that none of Christ's disciples ascribed to him the creation of the world, except John; that neither Paul, nor Matthew, nor Luke, nor Mark, have dared to call Jesus God; that John wrote later than the other evangelists, and at a time when a great number of men in the cities of Greece and Italy were converted; that he alludes to the conversion of Cornelius and of Sergius Paulus, to Peter's vision, to the circular letter sent by the apostles and elders at Jerusalem, which are all recorded in the Acts of the Apostles: by which quoting of the four Gospels and the Acts of the Apostles, and by quoting no other, Julian shows that these were the only historical books, received by Christians as of authority, and as the authentic memoirs of Jesus Christ, of his apostles, and of the doctrines taught by them. He himself expressly states the early date of these records; he calls them by the names which they now bear. He all along supposes, he nowhere attempts to question, their genuineness.

The argument in favour of the books of the New Testament, drawn from the notice taken of their contents by the early writers against the religion, is very considerable. It proves that the accounts which Christians had then were the accounts which we have now; that our present Scriptures were theirs. It proves, moreover, that neither Celsus in the second, Porphyry in the third, nor Julian in the fourth century, suspected the authenticity of these books. And when we consider how much it would have availed them to have cast a doubt upon this point, if they could: their concession upon the subject is extremely valuable.

## SECTION X

Formal catalogues of authentic Scriptures were published, in all which our present sacred histories were included.

This species of evidence comes later than the rest; as it was not natural that catalogues should be put forth until Christian writings became numerous; or until some writings showed themselves, claiming titles which did not belong to them, and thereby rendering it necessary to separate books of authority from others. But, when it does appear, it is extremely satisfactory; the catalogues, though numerous, and made in countries at a wide distance from one another, differing in nothing which is material, and all containing the four Gospels. To this last article there is no exception.

I. In the writings of Origen which remain, and in some extracts preserved by Eusebius, from works of his which are now lost, there are enumerations of the books of Scriptures, in which the Four Gospels and the Acts of the Apostles are distinctly specified, and in which no books appear beside what are now received. (Lardner, Cred. vol. iii. p. 234, et seq.; vol. viii. p. 196.)

II. Athanasias, about a century afterwards, delivered a catalogue of the books of the New Testament, containing our Scriptures and no others; of which he says, "In these alone the doctrine of Religion is taught; let no man add to them, or take anything from them." (Lardner, Cred. vol. ii. p. 223.)

III. About twenty years after Athanasius, Cyril, bishop of Jerusalem, set forth a catalogue of the books of Scripture exactly the same as ours, except that the "Revelation" is omitted. (Lardner, Cred. vol. ii. p. 270.)

IV. And fifteen years after Cyril, the council of Laodicea delivered an authoritative catalogue of canonical Scripture the same as ours with the omission of the "Revelation."

V. Catalogues now became frequent. From the year 363 to near the conclusion of the fourth century, we have catalogues by Epiphanius, (Lardner, Cred. vol. ii. p. 368.) by Gregory Nazianzen, by Philaster, bishop of Breseia in Italy, (Lardner, Cred. vol. ix. p. 132 & 373.) by Amphilochius, bishop of Iconium; all, for every purpose of historic evidence, the same as ours.

VI. Within the same period Jerome, the most learned Christian writer of his age, delivered a catalogue of the books of the New Testament, recognising every book now received, with a doubt concerning the Epistle to the Hebrews alone, and taking not the least notice of any book which is not now received. (Lardner, Cred. vol. x. p. 77.)

VII. Contemporary with Jerome, who lived in Palestine, was St. Augustine, in Africa, who published a catalogue, without joining to the Scriptures any other ecclesiastical writing, and without omitting one which we acknowledge. (Lardner, Cred. vol. x. p. 213.)

VIII. And with these concurs another writer, Rufen, presbyter of Aquileia, whose catalogue is perfect and unmixed, and concludes with these remarkable words: "These are the volumes which the fathers have included in the canon, and out of which they would have us prove the doctrine of our faith." (Lardner, Cred. vol. x. p. 187.)

## SECTION XI

These propositions cannot be predicated of any of those books which are commonly called Apocryphal Books of the New Testament.

There are many, who, hearing that various Gospels existed in ancient times under the names of the apostles, may have taken up a notion, that the selection of our present Gospels was an arbitrary choice. To these it may be very useful to know the truth of the case. I observe, therefore:—

I. That, beside our Gospels and the Acts of the Apostles, no Christian history, claiming to be written by an apostle or apostolical man, is quoted within three hundred years after the birth of Christ, by any writer now known; or, if quoted, is not quoted but with marks of censure and rejection.

I have not advanced this assertion without inquiry; and I doubt not but that the passages cited by Mr. Jones and Dr. Lardner; or a table, published in the year 1773, by the Rev. J. Atkinson, will make out the truth of the proposition. If there be any book which may seem to form an exception to the observation, it is a Hebrew Gospel, which was circulated under various titles. This Gospel is only once cited by Clemeus Alexandrinus, who lived in the latter part of the second century, and which same Clement quotes one or other of our four Gospels in almost every page of his work. It is also twice mentioned by Origen, A.D. 230; and both times with marks of diminution and discredit. And this is the ground upon which the exception stands. But this Gospel, in the main, agreed with our present Gospel of Saint Matthew.

Now if, with this account of the apocryphal Gospels, we compare what we have read concerning the canonical Scriptures in the preceding sections; or even recollect that general but well-founded assertion of Dr. Lardner, "That in the remaining works of Irenaeus, Clement of Alexandria, and Tertullian, who all lived in the first two centuries, there are more and larger quotations of the small volume of the New Testament than of all the works of Cicero, by writers of all characters, for several ages;" (Lardner, Cred. vol. xii. p. 53.) and if to this we add that we have, within the above-mentioned period, the remains of Christian writers who lived in Palestine, Syria, Asia Minor, Egypt, the part of Africa that used the Latin tongue, in Crete, Greece, Italy, and Gaul, in all which remains references are found to our evangelists; I apprehend that we shall perceive a clear and broad line of division between those writings and all others pretending to similar authority.

II. But beside certain histories which assumed the names of apostles, and which were forgeries, there were some other Christian writings, in the whole or in part of an historical nature, which are denominated apocryphal, as being of uncertain or of no authority.

Of this second class of writings, I have found only two which are noticed by any author of the first three centuries without express terms of condemnation: and these are, the one a book entitled the Preaching of Peter, quoted repeatedly by Clemens Alexandrinus, A.D. 196; the other a book entitled the Revelation of Peter, upon which Clemens Alexandrinus is said by Eusebius to have written notes; and which is twice cited in a work still extant, ascribed to the same author.

I conceive, therefore, that the proposition we have before advanced, even after it hath been subjected to every exception of every kind, separates our historical Scriptures from all other writings which profess to give an account of the same subject.

We may be permitted however to add,—

1. That there is no evidence that any spurious or apocryphal books existed in the first century of the Christian era, in which century all our historical books are proved to have been extant.

2. These apocryphal writings were not read in the churches of Christians;

3. Were not admitted into their volume;

4. Do not appear in their catalogues;

5. Were not noticed by their adversaries;

6. Were not alleged by different parties, as of authority in their controversies;

7. Were not the subjects, amongst them, of commentaries, versions, collections, expositions.

Finally, they were, with a consent nearly universal, reprobated by Christian writers of succeeding ages.

Although the books in question never obtained any degree of credit which can place them in competition with our Scriptures; yet it appears from the writings of the fourth century, that many such existed in that century, and in the century preceding it.

Perhaps the most probable explication is, that they were in general composed with a design of making a profit by the sale. It was an advantage taken of the pious curiosity of unlearned Christians. With a view to the same purpose, there were many of them adapted to the particular opinions of particular sects, which would naturally promote their circulation. Except the Gospel according to the Hebrews, there is none of which we hear more than the Gospel of the Egyptians; yet there is good reason to believe that Clement, a presbyter of Alexandria in Egypt, A.D. 184, and a man of almost universal reading, had never seen it. (Jones, vol. i. p. 243.) A Gospel according to Peter was another of the most ancient books of this kind; yet Serapion, bishop of Antioch, A.D. 200, had not read it, and speaks of obtaining a sight of this Gospel from some sectaries who used it. (Lardner, Cred. vol. ii. p. 557.) Even of the Gospel of the Hebrews, Jerome, at the end of the fourth century, was glad to procure a copy by the favour of the Nazarenes of Berea. Nothing of this sort ever happened concerning our Gospels.

One thing is observable of all the apocryphal Christian writings, viz. that they proceed upon the same fundamental history of Christ and his apostles as that which is disclosed in our Scriptures. The mission of Christ, his power of working miracles, his communication of that power to the apostles, his passion, death, and resurrection, are asserted by every one of them. The names under which some of them came forth are the names of men of eminence in our histories. The principal facts are supposed, the principal agents the same; which shows that these points were too much fixed to be altered or disputed.

If there be any book which appears to have imposed upon some considerable number of learned Christians, it is the Sibylline oracles. It was at that time universally understood that such a prophetic writing existed. Its contents were kept secret. This situation afforded to some one an opportunity to give out a writing under this name, favourable to the already established persuasion of Christians, and which writing, by the aid and recommendation of these circumstances, would in some degree, be received. Of the ancient forgery we know but little; what is now produced could not have imposed upon any one. It is nothing else than the Gospel history woven into verse.

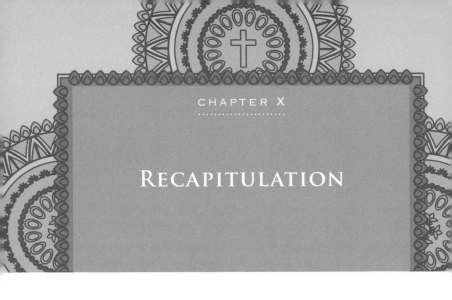

## CHAPTER X

# RECAPITULATION

The two points which form the subject of our present discussion are, first, that the Founder of Christianity, his associates, and immediate followers, passed their lives in labours, dangers, and sufferings; secondly, that they did so in attestation of the miraculous history recorded in our Scriptures, and solely in consequence of their belief of the truth of that history.

The argument, by which these two propositions have been maintained by us, stands thus:

The original propagators of Christianity voluntarily subjected themselves to lives of fatigue, danger, and suffering, in the prosecution of their undertaking. The nature of the undertaking; the character of the persons employed in it; the opposition of their tenets to the fixed opinions of the country in which they first advanced them; their condemnation of the religion of all other countries; their total want of power, authority, or force—render it in the highest degree probable that this must have been the case. The probability is increased by the fate of the Founder of the institution; and by what we also know of the cruel treatment of the converts to the institution, within thirty years after its commencement: both which points are attested by heathen writers, and leave it very incredible that the primitive emissaries of the religion should themselves escape with impunity. This probability, thus sustained by foreign testimony, is advanced to historical certainty, by the evidence of our own books; by the accounts of a writer who was the companion of the persons whose sufferings he relates; by the letters of the persons themselves; by predictions ascribed to the Founder of the religion; lastly, by incessant exhortations to fortitude and patience, and by an earnestness, repetition, and urgency upon the subject, which were unlikely to have appeared if there had not been some extraordinary call for the exercise of these virtues.

It is made out also with sufficient evidence, that both the teachers and converts of the religion, in consequence of their new profession, took up a new course of life and behaviour.

The next great question is, what they did this *for*. That it was for a miraculous story is extremely manifest; because, the designation that this particular person, Jesus of Nazareth, ought to be received as the Messiah, or as a messenger from God, they neither had, nor could have, anything but miracles to stand upon. That the exertions and sufferings of the apostles were for the story which we have now, is proved by the consideration that this story is transmitted to us by two of their own number, and by two others personally connected with them; that the particularity of the narrative proves that the writers claimed to possess circumstantial information, that from their situation they had full opportunity of acquiring such information, that they knew what their colleagues, their companions, their masters taught; that each of these books contains enough to prove the truth of the religion; that if any one of them therefore be genuine, it is sufficient; that the genuineness, however, of all of them is made out, as well by the general arguments which evince the genuineness of the most undisputed remains of antiquity, as also by peculiar and specific proofs ; by the distinguished regard paid by early Christians to the authority of these books; by an universal agreement with respect to these books, whilst doubts were entertained concerning some others; by contending sects appealing to them; by the early adversaries of the religion not disputing their genuineness, but, on the contrary, treating them as the depositaries of the history upon which the religion was founded; by many formal catalogues of these published in different and distant parts of the Christian world; lastly, by the absence or defect of the above-cited topics of evidence, when applied to any other histories of the same subject.

These are strong arguments to prove that the books actually proceeded from the authors whose names they bear; but the strict genuineness of the books is perhaps more than is necessary to the support of our proposition. For even supposing that, by reason of the silence of antiquity, or the loss of records, we knew not who were the writers of the four Gospels, yet the fact that they were received as authentic accounts of the transaction upon which the religion rested by Christians at or near the age of the apostles, by those whom the apostles had taught, and by societies which the apostles had founded; this fact, connected with the consideration that they are corroborative of each other's testimony, and that they are further corroborated by another contemporary history taking up the story where they had left it, and, in a narrative built upon that story, accounting for the rise and production of changes in the world, the effects of which subsist at this day; connected with the confirmation which they receive from letters written by the apostles themselves; and connected also with the reflection, that if the apostles delivered any different story it is lost; and that so great a change as the oblivion of one story and the substitution of another, under such circumstances, could not have taken place: this evidence would be deemed sufficient to prove concerning these books, that they exhibit the story which the apostles told, and for which, consequently, they acted and they suffered.

If it be so, the religion must be true. These men could not be deceivers. By only not bearing testimony, they might have avoided all these sufferings, and have lived quietly.

# PROPOSITION II

## THAT THERE IS NOT SATISFACTORY EVIDENCE, THAT PERSONS PRETENDING TO BE ORIGINAL WITNESSES OF ANY OTHER SIMILAR MIRACLES HAVE ACTED IN THE SAME MANNER, IN ATTESTATION OF THE ACCOUNTS WHICH THEY DELIVERED, AND SOLELY IN CONSEQUENCE OF THEIR BELIEF OF THE TRUTH OF THOSE ACCOUNTS

Our first proposition was, That there is satisfactory evidence that many pretending to be original witnesses of the Christian miracles, passed their lives in labours, dangers, and sufferings, voluntarily undertaken and undergone in attestation of the accounts which they delivered, and solely in consequence of their belief of the truth of those accounts; and that they also submitted, from the same motives, to new rules of conduct.

Our second proposition is That there is *not* satisfactory evidence, that persons pretending to be original witnesses of any other similar miracles have acted in the same manner, in attestation of the accounts which they delivered, and solely in consequence of their belief of the truth of those accounts.

If the founders of our religious sects since had undergone the life of toil and exertion, of danger and sufferings for a miraculous story; that is to say, if they had founded their public ministry upon the allegation of miracles wrought within their own knowledge, and upon narratives which could not be resolved into delusion or mistake; and if it had appeared that their conduct really had its origin in these accounts, I should have believed them. And my belief would be much strengthened, if the subject of the mission were of importance to the conduct and happiness of human life; if it testified anything which it behoved mankind to know from such authority; if the nature of what it delivered required the sort of proof which it alleged; if the occasion was adequate to the interposition, the end worthy of the means. In the last ease, my faith would be much confirmed if the effects of the transaction remained; more especially if a change had been wrought, at the time, in the opinion and conduct of such numbers as to lay the foundation of an institution, and of a system of doctrines, which had since overspread the greatest part of the civilized world. I should have believed the testimony; yet none of them do more than come up to the apostolic history.

In stating the comparison between our evidence, and what our adversaries may bring into competition with ours, we will divide the distinctions into two kinds,—those which relate to the proof, and those which relate to the miracles. Under the former head we may lay out of the case:—

I. Such accounts of supernatural events as are found only in histories by some ages posterior to the transaction; and of which it is evident that the historian could know little more than his reader. Ours is contemporary history. This difference alone removes the miraculous history of Pythagoras; the prodigies of Livy's history; the fables of the heroic ages; the whole of the Greek and Roman, as well as of the Gothic mythology; a great part of the legendary history of Popish saints. It applies also to the miracles of Apollonius Tyaneus. Also to some of the miracles of the third century, especially to one extraordinary instance, the account of Gregory, bishop of Neocesarea, called Thaumaturgus, delivered in the writings of Gregory of Nyssen.

II. We may lay out of the case accounts published in one country, of what passed in a distant country, without any proof that such accounts were known or received at home. In the case of Christianity, Judea was the centre of the mission. The story was published in the place in which it was acted. The church of Christ was first planted at Jerusalem itself.

III. We lay out of the case transient rumours. Upon the first publication of an extraordinary account, no one who is not personally acquainted with the transaction can know whether it be true or false, because any man may publish any story. It is in the future confirmation, or contradiction, of the account; in its permanency, or its disappearance; its increasing in notoriety; its being followed up by subsequent accounts, and being repeated in different and independent accounts—that solid truth is distinguished from fugitive lies. This distinction is altogether on the side of Christianity.

IV. We may lay out of the case what I call naked history. It has been said, that if the prodigies of the Jewish history had been found only in fragments of Manetho, or Berosus, we should have paid no regard to them: and I am willing to admit this. If we knew nothing of the fact, but from the fragment; if we possessed no proof that these accounts had been credited and acted upon, from times, probably, as ancient as the accounts themselves; if we had no visible effects connected with the history, no subsequent or collateral testimony to confirm it; under these circumstances I think that it would be undeserving of credit. But this certainly is not our case. It is properly a cumulation of evidence, by no means a naked or solitary record.

V. A mark of historical truth is particularity in names, dates, places, circumstances, and in the order of events preceding or following the transaction: of which kind, for instance, is the particularity in the description of St. Paul's shipwreck, in the 27th chapter of the Acts, which no man can read without being convinced that the writer was there; and also in the account of the cure of the blind man in the 9th chapter of St. John's Gospel, which bears every mark of personal knowledge on the part of the historian. Since, however, experience proves that particularity is not confined to truth, it is a proof of truth only to a certain extent, i. e. it reduces the question to whether we can depend or not upon the probity of the relater? which is a considerable advance in our present argument; for an express attempt to deceive, is charged upon the evangelists by few. If the historian acknowledge himself to have received his intelligence from others, the particularity of the narrative shows, prima facie, the accuracy of his inquiries, and the fulness of his information. Of the particularity which we allege, many examples may be found in all the Gospels.

VI. We lay out of the case such stories of supernatural events as require, on the part of the hearer, nothing more than an otiose assent. Such stories are credited more by the indolence of the hearer, than by his judgment: or, though not much credited, are passed from one to another without inquiry or resistance. To this case alone, belongs what is called the love of the marvellous. I have never known it carry men further. Men do not suffer persecution from the love of the marvellous. Of the indifferent nature we are speaking of are most vulgar errors and popular superstition. But not, surely, of this kind were the alleged miracles of Christ and his apostles. If a Jew took up the story, he found his darling partiality to his own nation and law wounded; if a Gentile, he found his idolatry and polytheism reprobated and condemned. Whoever entertained the account, whether Jew or Gentile, could not avoid the following reflection:—"If these things be true, I must give up the opinions and principles in which I have been brought up, the religion in which my fathers lived and died." It is not conceivable that a man should do this without being fully convinced of the truth and credibility of the narrative. But it did not stop at opinions. They who believed Christianity acted upon it. Many made it the express business of their lives to publish the intelligence. It was required of those who admitted that intelligence to change forthwith their conduct and their principles, and begin a new set of rules and system of behaviour.

If it be said, that the mere promise of a future state would do all this; I answer, that without any evidence to give credit or assurance to it, it would do nothing. If it be further said that men easily believe what they anxiously desire; in my opinion, the very contrary of this is nearer to the truth. Anxiety of desire, earnestness of expectation, the vastness of an event, rather causes men to disbelieve, to doubt, and to examine. When our Lord's resurrection was first reported to the apostles, they did not believe for joy. This was natural, and is agreeable to experience.

VII. We now also lay out of the case those which come merely in affirmance of opinions already formed. It has long been observed, that Popish miracles happen in Popish countries; that they make no converts; which proves that stories are accepted when they fall in with principles already fixed, which would not be attempted to be produced in the face of enemies, in opposition to reigning tenets, or when, if they be believed, the belief must draw men away from their preconceived and habitual opinions. In the former case, men may not only receive a miraculous account, but may both act and suffer on the side which the miracle supports, yet not act or suffer for the miracle, but in pursuance of a prior persuasion. The miracle, like any other argument which only confirms what was before believed, is admitted with little examination. In the moral, as in the natural world, it is change which requires a cause. The miracles of the Christian history were wrought in the midst of enemies, under a government, a priesthood, and a magistracy decidedly and vehemently adverse to them. They produced a change; they established a society upon the spot; they made converts; and those who were converted gave up to the testimony their most fixed opinions and most favourite prejudices. They who acted and suffered in the cause acted and suffered for the miracles: for there was no anterior persuasion to induce them. His miracles gave birth to his sect. It constitutes indeed a line of partition between the origin and the progress of Christianity. Frauds and fallacies might mix themselves with the progress, which could not possibly take place in the commencement of the religion. What should suggest to the first propagators of Christianity, especially to fishermen, tax-gatherers, and husbandmen, such a thought as that of changing the religion of the world; what could bear them through the difficulties in which the attempt engaged them; what could procure any degree of success to the attempt? are questions which apply, with great force, to the setting out of the institution—with less, to every future stage of it.

We may add that where miracles are alleged in affirmance of a prior opinion, they who believe the doctrine may sometimes propagate a belief of the miracles which they do not themselves entertain. This is the case of what are called pious frauds. It does not hold of the apostolical history. If the apostles did not believe the miracles, they did not believe the religion; and without this belief, what place was there for piety, in publishing and attesting miracles in its behalf? The truth is, that there is no assignable character which will account for the conduct of the apostles, supposing their story to be false. If bad men, what could have induced them to take such pains to promote virtue? If good men, they would not have gone about the country with a string of lies in their mouths.

In appreciating the credit of any miraculous story, these are distinctions which relate to the evidence. There are other distinctions, of great moment in the question, which relate to the miracles themselves.

I. It is not necessary to admit as a miracle what can be resolved into a false perception. Of this nature was the demon of Socrates; the visions of Saint Anthony, and of many others. All these may be accounted for by a momentary insanity. They are, for the most part, cases of visions or voices. The object is hardly ever touched. One sense does not confirm another. They are likewise almost always cases of a solitary witness. Lastly, these are always cases of miracles of which the whole existence is of short duration, in contradistinction to miracles which are attended with permanent effects. The sensible proof is gone when the apparition or sound is over. But if a person born blind be restored to sight, a notorious cripple to the use of his limbs, or a dead man to life, here is a permanent effect produced by supernatural means. The man cured or restored is there: his former condition was known, and his present condition may be examined. This can by no possibility be resolved into false perception: and of this kind are by far the greater part of the miracles recorded in the New Testament. The blind man whose restoration to sight at Jerusalem is recorded in the ninth chapter of Saint John's

Gospel did not quit the place or conceal himself from inquiry. On the contrary, he was forthcoming to satisfy the scrutiny, and to sustain the browbeating of Christ's angry and powerful enemies. This, therefore, could not be the effect of any momentary delirium, either in the subject or in the witnesses of the transaction. There are other cases of a mixed nature, in which, although the principal miracle be momentary, some circumstance combined with it is permanent. Of this kind is the history of Saint Paul's conversion. (Acts ix.) The sudden vision and the voice upon the road to Damascus, were momentary: but Paul's blindness for three days; the communication made to Ananias in another place, and by a vision independent of the former; Ananias finding out Paul in the condition described in consequence of intelligence so received, and Paul's recovery of his sight upon Ananias laying his hands upon him; are circumstances which take the transaction entirely out of the case of momentary miracles. Exactly the same thing may be observed of Peter's vision preparatory to the call of Cornelius. The vision might be a dream; the message could not. Either communication taken separately, might be a delusion; the concurrence of the two was impossible to happen without a supernatural cause.

Beside the risk of delusion which attaches upon momentary miracles, there is also much more room for imposture. The account cannot be examined at the moment: and when that is also a moment of hurry and confusion, it may not be difficult for men of influence to gain credit to any story which they may wish to have believed. This is precisely the case of the appearance of Castor and Pollux in the battle fought by Posthumius with the Latins at the lake Regillus. Posthumius, after the battle, spread the report of such an appearance. No person could say with positiveness what was or what was not seen amidst the tumult of a battle.

In assigning false perceptions as the origin of miraculous accounts, I have not mentioned claims to inspiration, illuminations, secret notices or directions, internal sensations, or consciousnesses of being acted upon by spiritual influences, good or bad, because these, appealing to no external proof, form no part of what can be accounted miraculous evidence. The discussion, therefore, of all such pretensions may be omitted.

II. It is not necessary to bring into the comparison what may be called tentative miracles; that is, where, out of a great number of trials, some succeed; and in the accounts of which enough is stated to show that the cases produced are only a few out of many. This observation bears with considerable force upon the ancient oracles and auguries. It is also applicable to the cures wrought by relics, and at the tombs of saints. No solution of this sort is applicable to the miracles of the Gospel. There is nothing in the narrative which can induce, or even allow, us to believe, that Christ attempted cures in many instances, and succeeded in a few; or that he ever made the attempt in vain. He did not profess to heal everywhere all that were sick; on the contrary, he told the Jews, evidently meaning to represent his own case, that, "although many widows were in Israel in the days of Elias, when the heaven was shut up three years and six months, when great famine was throughout all the land, yet unto none of them was Elias sent, save unto Sarepta, a city of Sidon, unto a woman that was a widow:" and that "many lepers were in Israel in the time of Eliseus the prophet, and none of them was cleansed saving Naaman the Syrian." (Luke iv. 25.) By which examples he gave them to understand, that it was not the nature of a Divine interposition to be general; still less to answer every challenge that might be made, which would teach men to put their faith upon these experiments. Christ never pronounced the word, but the effect followed.*

We may observe, also, that many of the cures which Christ wrought, such as that of a person blind from his birth; also raising the dead, walking upon the sea, feeding a great multitude with a few loaves and fishes, are of a nature which does not admit of the supposition of a fortunate experiment.

---

*One, and only one, instance may be produced in which the disciples of Christ do seem to have attempted a cure, and not to have been able to perform it. The story is very ingenuously related by three of the evangelists. (Matt. xvii. 14. Mark ix. 14. Luke ix. 33.) The patient was afterwards healed by Christ himself; and the whole transaction seems to have been intended to display the superiority of Christ above all who performed miracles in his name, a distinction which it might be necessary to inculcate by some such proof as this.

III. We may dismiss from the question all accounts in which, allowing the phenomenon to be real, the fact to be true, it still remains doubtful whether a miracle were wrought. This is the case with the ancient history of what is called the thundering legion, of the extraordinary circumstances which obstructed the rebuilding of the temple at Jerusalem by Julian; the circling of the flames and fragrant smell at the martyrdom of Polycarp; the sudden shower that extinguished the fire into which the Scriptures were thrown in the Diocletian persecution; Constantine's dream; his inscribing in consequence of it the cross upon his standard and the shields of his soldiers; his victory, and the escape of the standard-bearer; perhaps, also, the imagined appearance of the cross in the heavens. It is a doubt, likewise, which ought to be excluded from those narratives which relate to the supernatural cure of hypochondriacal and nervous complaints, and of all diseases which are much affected by the imagination. The miracles of the second and third century are, usually, healing the sick and casting out evil spirits, miracles in which there is room for some error and deception. (Jortin's Remarks, vol. ii. p. 51.)

IV. To the same head of objection, may also be referred accounts in which the variation of a small circumstance may have transformed some extraordinary appearance, or some critical coincidence of events, into a miracle. The miracles of the Gospel can by no possibility be explained away in this manner. The feeding of the five thousand with a few loaves and fishes surpasses all bounds of exaggeration. The raising of Lazarus, of the widow's son at Nain, as well as many of the cures which Christ wrought, come not within the compass of misrepresentation.

Having thus enumerated several exceptions which may justly be taken to relations of miracles, it is necessary, when we read the Scriptures, to bear in our minds that although there be miracles recorded in the New Testament, which fall within some of the exceptions here assigned, yet they are united with others, to which none of the same exceptions extend, and that their credibility stands upon this union. Thus the visions and revelations which Saint Paul asserts to have been imparted to him were attested by external miracles wrought by himself, and by miracles wrought in the cause to which these visions relate. This is not ordinarily true of the visions of enthusiasts, or even of the accounts in which they are contained. Whatever objection, we have numerous miracles which are free from it; and even those to which it is applicable are little affected by it in their credit, because there are few who, admitting the rest, will reject them.

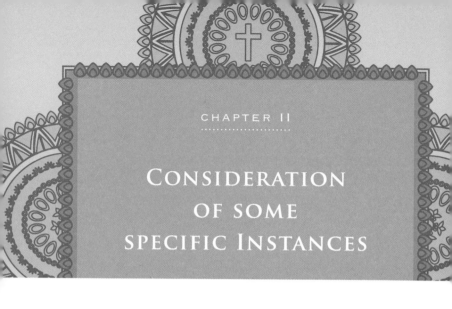

## CHAPTER II

# CONSIDERATION OF SOME SPECIFIC INSTANCES

B ut they with whom we argue have a right to select their own examples. The instances with which Mr. Hume has chosen to confront the miracles of the New Testament, and which, therefore, we are entitled to regard as the strongest which the history could supply, are the three following:

I. The cure of a blind and of a lame man of Alexandria, by the emperor Vespasian, as related by Tacitus;

II. The restoration of the limb of an attendant in a Spanish church, as told by Cardinal de Retz; and,

III. The cures said to be performed at the tomb of the abbe Paris in the early part of the eighteenth century.

I. The narrative of Tacitus is delivered in these terms: "One of the common people of Alexandria, known to be diseased in his eyes, by the admonition of the god Serapis, whom that superstitious nation worship above all other gods, prostrated himself before the emperor, earnestly imploring from him a remedy for his blindness, and entreating that he would deign to anoint with his spittle his cheeks and the balls of his eyes. Another, diseased in his hand, requested, by the admonition of the same god, that he might be touched by the foot of the emperor. Vespasian at first derided and despised their application; afterwards, when they continued to urge their petitions, he sometimes appeared to dread the imputation of vanity; at other times, by the earnest supplication of the patients, and the persuasion of his flatterers, to be induced to hope for success. At length he commanded an inquiry to be made by the physicians, whether such a blindness and debility were vincible by human aid. The report of the physicians contained various points: that in the one, the power of vision was not destroyed, but would return if the obstacles were removed; that in the other, the diseased joints might be restored, if a healing power were applied; that it was, perhaps, agreeable to the gods to do this; that the emperor was elected by divine assistance; lastly, that the credit of the success would be the emperor's, the ridicule of the disappointment would fall upon the patients. Vespasian believing that everything was in the power of his fortune, and that nothing was any longer incredible, whilst the multitude which stood by eagerly expected the event, with a countenance expressive of joy, executed what he was desired to do. Immediately the hand was restored to its use, and light returned to the blind man. They who were present relate both these cures, even at this time, when there is nothing to be gained by lying." (Tacit. Hist. lib. iv.)

Now, though Tacitus wrote this account twenty-seven years after the miracle, and wrote at Rome of what passed at Alexandria, and wrote also from report; and although it does not appear that he had examined the story or that he believed it, yet I think his testimony sufficient to prove that the two men in question did apply to Vespasian; that Vespasian did touch the diseased in the manner related; and that a cure was reported to have followed the operation. But the affair labours under a just suspicion, that it was a concerted imposture brought about by collusion between the patients, the physician, and the emperor. There was everything to suggest and facilitate such a scheme. The miracle was calculated to confer honour upon the emperor, and upon the god Serapis. It was achieved in the midst of the emperor's followers; in a city and amongst a populace before-hand devoted to the worship of the god. And the report of the physicians is just such a report as would have been made of a case in which no external marks of the disease existed, and which, consequently, was capable of being easily counterfeited. The strongest circumstance in Tacitus's narration is, that the first patient was "notus tabe oculorum," notorious for the disease in his eyes. But this was a circumstance which might have found its way into the story in its progress; or it might be true that the malady of the eyes was notorious, yet that the nature and degree of the disease had never been ascertained. The emperor's reserve was easily affected: or it is possible he might not be in the secret. To have brought this supposed miracle within the limits of comparison with the miracles of Christ, it ought to have appeared that a person of a low station, in the midst of enemies, with the whole power of the country opposing him, pretended to perform these cures, and required the spectators, upon the strength of what they saw, to give up their firmest hopes and opinions, and follow him through a life of trial and danger; that many were so moved as to obey his call, at the expense of every notion in which they had been brought up, and of their ease, safety, and reputation; and that by these beginnings a change was produced in the world: a case very unlike anything we find in Tacitus's relation.

II. The story taken from the Memoirs of Cardinal de Retz, which is the second example alleged by Mr. Hume, is this: "In the church of Saragossa in Spain, the canons showed me a man whose business it was to light the lamps; telling me, that he had been several years at the gate with one leg only. I saw him with two." (Liv. iv. A.D. 1654.)

It is stated by Mr. Hume, that the cardinal who relates this story did not believe it; and it nowhere appears that he either examined the limb, or asked any one a single question about the matter. An artificial leg would be sufficient, in a place where no such contrivance had ever before been heard of, to give origin and currency to the report. The ecclesiastics of the place would, it is probable, favour the story, inasmuch as it advanced the honour of their image and church. And if they patronized it, no other person at Saragossa would care to dispute it. If, as I have suggested, the contrivance of an artificial limb was then new, it would not occur to the cardinal himself to suspect it; especially under the carelessness of mind with which he heard the tale, and the little inclination he felt to scrutinize its fallacy.

III. The miracles related to have been wrought at the tomb of the abbe Paris admit in general of this solution. The patients who frequented the tomb were so affected by their devotion, their expectation, the place, the solemnity, and by the sympathy of the surrounding multitude, that many of them were thrown into violent convulsions, which in certain instances, produced a removal of disorder, depending upon obstruction. The report of the French physicians upon that mysterious remedy is very applicable to the present consideration, viz. that the pretenders to the art, by working upon the imaginations of their patients, were frequently able to produce convulsions.

Circumstances which indicate this explication, in the case of the Parisian miracles, are the following:

1. They were tentative. Out of many thousand sick, infirm, and diseased persons who resorted

to the tomb, the professed history of the miracles contains only nine cures.

2. The convulsions at the tomb are admitted.

3. The diseases were, for the most part, of that sort which depends upon inaction and obstruction, as dropsies, palsies, and some tumours.

4. The cures were gradual; some patients attending many days, some several weeks, and some several months.

5. The cures were many of them incomplete.

6. Others were temporary.

So that all the wonder we are called upon to account for is, that out of an almost innumerable multitude which resorted to the tomb for the cure of their complaints, and many of whom were there agitated by strong convulsions, a very small proportion experienced a beneficial change in their constitution, especially in the action of the nerves and glands.

Some of the cases alleged do not require that we should have recourse to this solution. The first case is scarcely distinguishable from the progress of a natural recovery. It was that of a young man who laboured under an inflammation of one eye. The inflamed eye was relieved. The inflammation had before been abated by medicine; and the young man, at the time of his attendance at the tomb, was using a lotion of laudanum. And, the inflammation, after some interval, returned. Another case was that of a young man who had lost his sight by the puncture of an awl, and the discharge of the aqueous humour through the wound. The sight, which had been gradually returning, was much improved during his visit to the tomb, that is, probably in the same degree in which the discharged humour was replaced by fresh secretions. And these two are the only cases which, from their nature, should seem unlikely to be affected by convulsions.

These are the strongest examples which the history of ages supplies.

PART II

# OF THE AUXILIARY EVIDENCES OF CHRISTIANITY

## CHAPTER 1

# PROPHECY

Isaiah iii. 13; liii. "Behold, my servant shall deal prudently; he shall be exalted and extolled, and be very high. As many were astonished at thee; his visage was so marred more than any man, and his form more than the sons of men: so shall he sprinkle many nations; the kings shall shut their mouths at him: for that which had not been told them shall they see; and that which they had not heard shall they consider. Who hath believed our report? and to whom is the arm of the Lord revealed? For he shall grow up before him as a tender plant, and as a root out of a dry ground: he hath no form nor comeliness; and when we shall see him, there is no beauty that we should desire him. He is despised and rejected of men, a man of sorrows, and acquainted with grief: and we hid, as it were, our faces from him: he was despised, and we esteemed him not. Surely he hath borne our griefs, and carried our sorrows: yet we did esteem him stricken, smitten of God, and afflicted. But he was wounded for our transgressions, he was bruised for our iniquities, the chastisement of our peace was upon him; and with his stripes we are healed. All we like sheep have gone astray; we have turned every one to his own way; and the Lord hath laid on him the iniquity of us all. He was oppressed, and he was afflicted, yet he opened not his mouth: he is brought as a lamb to the slaughter, and as a sheep before her shearers is dumb, so he opened not his mouth. He was taken from prison and from judgment; and who shall declare his generation? for he was cut off out of the land of the living: for the transgression of my people was he stricken. And he made his grave with the wicked, and with the rich in his death; because he had done no violence, neither was any deceit in his mouth. Yet it pleased the Lord to bruise him; he hath put him to grief. When thou shalt make his soul an offering for sin, he shall see his seed, he shall prolong his days, and the pleasure of the Lord shall prosper in his hand. He shall see of the travail of his soul, and shall be satisfied: by his knowledge shall my righteous servant justify many; for he shall bear their iniquities. Therefore will I divide him a portion with the great, and he shall divide the spoil with the strong; because he hath poured out his soul unto death; and he was numbered with the transgressors, and he bare the sin of many, and made intercession for the transgressors."

These words are the predictions of a writer who lived seven centuries before the Christian era.

That the words alleged were actually spoken or written before the fact to which they are applied took place, or could by any natural means be foreseen, is, in the present instance, incontestable. The record comes out of the custody of adversaries. The Jews, as an ancient father well observed, are our librarians. The passage is in their copies as well as in ours. With many attempts to explain it away, none has ever been made by them to discredit its authenticity.

And what adds to the force of the quotation is, that it is taken from writing declaredly prophetic. The words of Isaiah were delivered by him in a prophetic character. The public sentiments of the Jews concerning the design of Isaiah's writings are set forth in the book of Ecclesiasticus:* "He saw by an excellent spirit what should come to pass at the last, and he comforted them that mourned in Sion. He showed what should come to pass for ever, and secret things or ever they came."

The application of the prophecy to the evangelic history is plain and appropriate. The obscurities are few, and not of great importance. Nor have I found that varieties of reading produce any material alteration in the sense of the prophecy.

There is good proof that the ancient Rabbins explained it of their expected Messiah:+ but their modern expositors concur in representing it as a description of the calamitous

---

* Chap. xlviii. ver. 24.

+ Hulse, Theol. Jud. p. 430.

state, and intended restoration, of the Jewish people, who are here, as they say, exhibited under the character of a single person.

The clause in the ninth verse, which we render "for the transgression of my people was he stricken," and in the margin, "was the stroke upon him," the Jews read "for the transgression of my people was the stroke upon them." The Hebrew pronoun is capable of a plural as well as of a singular signification.* And this is all the variation contended for; the rest of the prophecy they read as we do. The application which the Jews contend for appears to me to labour under insuperable difficulties; in particular, it may be demanded of them to explain in whose name or person, if the Jewish people he the sufferer, does the prophet speak, when he says, "He hath borne our griefs, and carried our sorrows, yet we did esteem him stricken, smitten of God, and afflicted; but he was wounded for our transgressions, he was bruised for our iniquities, the chastisement of our peace was upon him, and with his stripes we are healed." Again, the description in the seventh verse, "he was oppressed and he was afflicted, yet he opened not his mouth; he is brought as a lamb to the slaughter, and as a sheep before her shearers is dumb, so he opened not his

---

* Bishop Lowth adopts in this place the reading of the seventy, which gives smitten to death, "for the transgression of my people was he smitten to death." The addition of the words "to death" makes an end of the Jewish interpretation of the clause.

mouth," quadrates with no part of the Jewish history with which we are acquainted. The mention of the "grave" and the "tomb," in the ninth verse, is not very applicable to the fortunes of a nation; and still less so is the conclusion of the prophecy, which expressly represents the sufferings as voluntary, and the sufferer as interceding for the offenders; "because he hath poured out his soul unto death, and he was numbered with the transgressors, and he bare the sin of many, and made intercession for the transgressors."

There are other prophecies of the Old Testament which are deserving of regard and consideration: but I content myself with stating the above, as well because I think it the clearest and the strongest.

II. A second head of argument from prophecy is founded upon our Lord's predictions concerning the destruction of Jerusalem, recorded by three out of the four evangelists.

Luke xxi. 5–25. "And as some spake of the temple, how it was adorned with goodly stones and gifts, he said, As for these things which ye behold, the days will come in which there shall not be left one stone upon another, that shall not be thrown down. And they asked him, saying, Master, but when shall these things be? and what sign will there be when these things shall come to pass? And he said, Take heed that ye be not deceived; for many shall come in my name, saying, I am Christ; and the time draweth near; go ye not therefore after them. But when ye shall hear of wars and commotions, be not terrified: for these things must first come to pass; but the end is not by-and-by. Then said he unto them, Nation shall rise against nation, and kingdom against kingdom; and great earth-quakes shall be in divers places, and famines and pestilences; and fearful sights, and great signs shall there be from heaven. But before all these, they shall lay their hands on you, and persecute you, delivering you up to the synagogues, and into prisons, being brought before kings and rulers for my name's sake. And it shall turn to you for a testimony. Settle it therefore in your hearts not to meditate before what ye shall answer: for I will give you a mouth and wisdom, which all your adversaries shall not be able to gainsay nor resist. And ye shall be betrayed both by parents, and brethren, and kinsfolk, and friends; and some of you shall they cause to be put to death. And ye shall be hated of all men for my name's sake. But there shall not an hair of your head perish. In your patience possess ye your souls. And when ye shall see Jerusalem compassed with armies, then know that the desolation thereof is nigh. Then let them which are in Judea flee to the mountains; and let them which are in the midst of it depart out; and let not them that are in the countries enter thereinto. For these be the days of vengeance, that all things which are written may be fulfilled. But woe unto them that are with child and to them that give suck in those days: for there shall be great distress in the land, and wrath upon this people. And they shall fall by the edge of the sword, and shall be led away captive into all nations: and Jerusalem shall be trodden down by the Gentiles, until the times of the Gentiles be fulfilled."

In terms nearly similar, this discourse is related in the twenty-fourth chapter of Matthew and the thirteenth of Mark. The prospect of the same evils drew from our Saviour, on another occasion, the following expressions of concern, which are preserved by St. Luke (xix. 41–44): "And when he was come near, he beheld the city and wept over it, saying, If thou hadst known, even thou, at least in this thy day, the things which belong unto thy peace! but now they are hid from thine eyes. For the day shall come upon thee, that thine enemies shall cast a trench about thee, and compass thee round and keep thee in on every side, and shall lay thee even with the ground, and thy children within thee; and they shall not leave in thee one stone upon another; because thou knowest not the time of thy visitation"—These passages are direct and explicit predictions. References to the same event are found in divers other discourses of our Lord. (Matt. xxi. 33–46; xxii. 1–7. Mark xii. 1–12. Luke xiii. 1–9; xx. 9–20; xxi. 5–13.)

The general agreement of the description with the ruin of the Jewish nation, and the capture of Jerusalem under Vespasian, thirty-six years after Christ's death, has been shown by many learned writers. The only question which can be raised upon the subject is, whether the prophecy was really delivered before the event?

1. The judgment of antiquity, though varying in the precise year of the publication of the three Gospels, concurs in assigning them a date prior

to the destruction of Jerusalem. (Lardner, vol. xiii.)

2.  The destruction of Jerusalem took place in the seventieth year after the birth of Christ. The three evangelists were, it is probable, not much younger than he was. They must have been far advanced in life when Jerusalem was taken; and no reason has been given why they should defer writing their histories so long.

3.  (Le Clerc, Diss. III. de Quat. Evang. num. vii. p. 541.) If the evangelists, at the time of writing the Gospels, had known of the destruction of Jerusalem, it is most probable that they would have dropped some word or other about the completion; in like manner as Luke, after relating the denunciation of a dearth by Agabus, adds, "which came to pass in the days of Claudius Caesar;" (Acts xi. 28.) whereas the prophecies are given distinctly in each of the first three Gospels, and referred to in several different passages of each, and in none of all these places does there appear the smallest intimation that the things spoken of had come to pass. I do admit that it would have been the part of an impostor, who wished his readers to believe that this book was written before the event, when in truth it was written after it, to have suppressed any

such intimation carefully. But this was not the character of the authors of the Gospel.

4. The admonitions* which Christ is represented to have given to his followers to save themselves by flight are not easily accounted for on the supposition of the prophecy being fabricated after the event. Either the Christians did make their escape from Jerusalem, or they did not: if they did, they must have had the prophecy amongst them: if they did not know of any such prediction, it was an improbable fiction, in a writer publishing his work near to that time and addressing his work to Jews and to Jewish converts to state that the followers of Christ had received admonition of which they made no use when the occasion arrived.

5. If the prophecies had been composed after the event, there would have been more specification.

---

* "When ye shall see Jerusalem compassed with armies, then know that the desolation thereof is nigh; then let them which are in Judea flee to the mountains; then let them which are in the midst of it depart out, and let not them that are in the countries enter thereinto."—Luke xxi. 20, 21. "When ye shall see Jerusalem compassed with armies, then let them which be in Judea flee unto the mountains; let him which is on the house-top not come down to take anything out of his house; neither let him which is in the field return back to take his clothes."—Matt. xiv. 18.

The names or descriptions of the enemy, the general, the emperor, would have been found in them. The counterfeited prophecies of the Sibylline oracles, of the twelve patriarchs, and, most others of the kind, are mere transcripts of the history, moulded into a prophetic form.

It is objected that the prophecy of the destruction of Jerusalem is connected with expressions which relate to the final judgment of the world. To which I answer, that the objection does not concern our present argument. If our Saviour actually foretold the destruction of Jerusalem, it is sufficient.

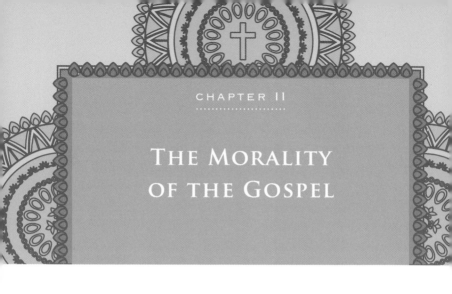

## CHAPTER II

# THE MORALITY
# OF THE GOSPEL

I n stating the morality of the Gospel as an argument of its truth, I am willing to admit that the teaching of morality was not the primary design of the mission; secondly, that morality, neither in the Gospel, nor in any other book, can be a subject of discovery.

If I were to describe in a very few words the scope of Christianity as a revelation,* I should say that it was to influence the conduct of human life, by establishing

---

* Great and beneficial effects may accrue from the mission of Christ, and especially from his death, which do not belong to Christianity as a revelation. I think it is a general opinion that the beneficial effects of Christ's death extend to the whole human species. It was the redemption of the world. "He is the propitiation for our sins, and not for ours only, but for the whole world;" 1. John ii. 2. Probably the future happiness, perhaps the future existence of

the proof of a future state of reward and punishment,—
"to bring life and immortality to light." The direct object,
therefore, is to supply motives, and not rules. The members of civilised society can, in all ordinary cases, judge how
they ought to act: but without credited evidence of a future
state, they want strength of motive sufficient to bear up
against the force of passion, and the temptation of present
advantage. Their rules want authority. The most important
service, and which one might expect beforehand would be
the great office of a revelation from God, is to convey to
the world authorised assurances of the reality of a future
existence. And although in doing this moral precepts may
be occasionally given, yet still they do not form the original
purpose of the mission.

Secondly; morality, neither in the Gospel nor in any
other book, can be a subject of discovery. There cannot, in
morality, be anything similar to what are called discoveries in natural philosophy, in the arts of life, and in some
sciences; as the system of the universe, the circulation of
the blood, the polarity of the magnet, the laws of gravi-
tation, alphabetical writing, decimal arithmetic, and some
other things of the same sort; facts, or proofs, before totally
unknown and unthought of. Whoever, therefore, expects in

---

the species, and more gracious terms of acceptance extended to all, might
depend upon it. Now these effects do not belong to Christianity as a
revelation; because they exist with respect to those to whom it is not
revealed.

reading the New Testament to be struck with discoveries in morals in the manner in which his mind was affected when he first came to the knowledge of the discoveries above mentioned; expects the impossible.

When it is once settled that to do good is virtue, the rest is calculation. But since the calculation cannot be instituted concerning each particular action, we establish intermediate rules; concerning our actions, we have only to ask whether they be agreeable to the rules. Now, in the formation of these rules, there is no place for discovery, but there is ample room for the exercise of wisdom, judgment, and prudence.

As I wish to deliver argument, I shall treat of the morality of the Gospel in subjection to these observations.

The division under which the subject may be most conveniently treated is that of the things taught, and the manner of teaching.

Under the first head, I should willingly transcribe the whole of what has been said by the author of The Internal Evidence of Christianity; because it is impossible to say the same things so well. This acute observer of human nature, and sincere convert to Christianity, appears to me to have made out satisfactorily the two following positions, viz.—

I. That the Gospel omits some qualities which have usually engaged the admiration of mankind, but which, in reality, have been Prejudicial to human happiness.

II. That the Gospel has brought forward some
virtues which possess the highest intrinsic
value, but which have commonly been
overlooked and condemned.

The first of these propositions he exemplifies in the
instances of friendship, patriotism, active courage.

The second, in the instances of passive courage or
endurance of sufferings, patience under affronts and inju-
ries, humility, irresistance, placability.

There are two opposite descriptions of character under
which mankind may generally be classed. The one possesses
rigour, firmness, resolution; is daring and active, quick in its
sensibilities, jealous of its fame, eager in its attachments,
inflexible in its purpose, violent in its resentments.

The other meek, yielding, complying, forgiving; not
prompt to act, but willing to suffer; silent and gentle under
rudeness and insult, suing for reconciliation where others
would demand satisfaction, giving way to the pushes of
impudence, conceding and indulgent to the prejudices, the
wrong-headedness, the intractability of those with whom
it has to deal.

The former of these characters is, and ever hath been,
the favourite of the world. It is the character of great men.
There is a dignity in it which universally commands respect.

The latter is poor-spirited, tame, and abject. Yet with
the Founder of Christianity this latter is the subject of
his commendation, his precepts, his example. This is the

character designed in the following remarkable passages: "Resist not evil: but whosoever shall smite thee on the right cheek, turn to him the other also; and if any man will sue thee at the law, and take away thy coat, let him have thy cloak also: and whosoever shall compel thee to go a mile, go with him twain: love your enemies, bless them that curse you, do good to them that hate you, and pray for them which despitefully use you and persecute you." This certainly is not commonplace morality. It is very original. It shows at least that no two things can be more different than the Heroic and the Christian characters.

Now the author to whom I refer has proved that the latter character possesses the most of true worth, both as being most difficult to be acquired or sustained, and as contributing most to the happiness and tranquillity of social life. The state of his argument is as follows:

I. If this disposition were universal, the case is clear; the world would be a society of friends. Whereas, if the other disposition were universal, it would produce a scene of universal contention.

II. If, what is the fact, the disposition be partial; in whatever degree it does prevail, in the same proportion it prevents, allays, and terminates quarrels, the great disturbers of human happiness, and the great sources of human misery.

Without this disposition enmities must not
only be frequent, but, once begun, eternal:
for, each retaliation being a fresh injury, and
consequently requiring a fresh satisfaction, no
period can be assigned to the reciprocation of
affronts, but that which closes the lives of the
parties.

Although the former of the two characters above
described may be occasionally useful; and these may be
instruments of important benefits to mankind, yet is this
nothing more than what is true of many qualities which are
acknowledged to be vicious. Envy is a quality of this sort:
many a scholar, many an artist, many a soldier, has been
produced by it; nevertheless, since in its general effects it is
noxious, it is properly condemned by sober moralists.

It was a portion of the same character, which our
Saviour displayed in his repeated correction of the ambi-
tion of his disciples; his frequent admonitions that great-
ness with them was to consist in humility; his censure of
that love of distinction which the chief persons amongst his
countrymen were wont to betray.

The precepts we have tired relate to personal conduct
from personal motives; to cases in which men act from
impulse, for themselves and from themselves. When it
comes to be considered what is necessary to be done for the
sake of the public, and out of a regard to the general welfare, it comes to a case to which the rules do not belong.

II. A second argument, drawn from the morality of the New Testament, is the stress which is laid by our Saviour upon the regulation of the thoughts.

"Out of the heart proceed evil thoughts, murders, adulteries, fornications," &c. "These are the things which defile a man." (Matt. xv. 19.)

"Wo unto you, Scribes and Pharisees, hypocrites! for ye make clean the outside of the cup and of the platter, but within they are full of extortion and excess.—Ye are like unto whited sepulchres, which indeed appear beautiful outward, but are within full of dead men's bones, and of all uncleanness; even so ye also outwardly appear righteous unto men, but within ye are full of hypocrisy and iniquity." (Matt. xxiii. 25, 27)

And more particularly that strong expression, (Matt. v. 28.) "Whosoever looketh on a woman to lust after her, hath committed adultery with her already in his heart."

The propensities of our nature must be subject to regulation; but the question is, where the check ought to be placed, upon the thought, or only upon the action? In this question our Saviour has pronounced a decisive judgment. He makes the control of thought essential. Now I contend that this is the only discipline which can succeed. Boerhaave, speaking of this very declaration of our Saviour, "Whosoever looketh on a woman to lust after her, hath already committed adultery with her in his heart," and understanding it, as we do, to contain an injunction to lay the check upon the thoughts, was wont to say that "our

Saviour knew mankind better than Socrates." Hailer, who has recorded this saying of Boerhaave, adds to it the following remarks of his own:—(Letters to his Daughter.) "It did not escape the observation of our Saviour that the rejection of any evil thoughts was the best defence against vice: for when a debauched person fills his imagination with impure pictures, the licentious ideas which he recalls fail not to stimulate his desires with a degree of violence which he cannot resist. This will be followed by gratification, unless some external obstacle should prevent him from the commission of a sin which he had internally resolved on." I suppose these reflections will be generally assented to.

III. Thirdly, had a teacher of morality been asked concerning a general principle of conduct; and had he instructed the person who consulted him, "constantly to refer his actions to what he believed to be the will of his Creator, and constantly to have in view not his own interest and gratification alone, but the happiness and comfort of those about him," he would have been thought to have delivered a judicious answer; because he suggested the only motive which acts steadily and uniformly; and in the second he corrected what of all tendencies in the human character stands most in need of correction, selfishness. In estimating the value of a moral rule, we are to have regard not only to the particular duty, but the general spirit. So, the rule here recited will never fail to make him who obeys it considerate not only of the rights, but of the feelings of other men.

Now what, in the most applauded philosopher of the most enlightened age, would have been deemed worthy of his wisdom to say, our Saviour hath said.

"Then one of them, which was a lawyer, asked him a question, tempting him, and saying, Master, which is the great commandment in the law? Jesus said unto him, Thou shalt love the Lord thy God with all thy heart, and with all thy soul, and with all thy mind; this is the first and great commandment: and the second is like unto it, Thou shalt love thy neighbour as thyself: on these two commandments hang all the law and the prophets." (Matt. xxii. 35–40.)

The second precept occurs in St. Matthew (xix. 16); and both of them, in Luke (x. 27). In these two latter instances the question proposed was, "What shall I do to inherit eternal life?"

Upon all these occasions I consider the words of our Saviour as expressing precisely the same thing as what I have put into the mouth of the moral philosopher. Nor do I think that it detracts from the merit of the answer, that these precepts are extant in the Mosaic code: for his stating of them as the greatest and the sum of all the others; was our Saviour's own.

And it is so well known as to require no citations to verify it, that this regard to the welfare of others, runs in various forms through all the preceptive parts of the apostolic writings.

This sacred principle, this earnest recommendation of forbearance, lenity, and forgiveness, mixes with all the writings of that age. There are more quotations in the apostolical fathers of texts which relate to these points than of any other. Christ's sayings had struck them. "Not rendering," said Polycarp, the disciple of John, "evil for evil, or railing for railing, or striking for striking, or cursing for cursing." Again, speaking of some whose behaviour had given great offence, "Be ye moderate," says he, "on this occasion, and look not upon such as enemies, but call them back as suffering and erring members, that ye save your whole body." (Pol. Ep. ad Phil. c. 2 & 11.)

IV. A fourth quality by which the morality of the Gospel is distinguished is the exclusion of regard to fame and reputation.

> "Take heed that ye do not your alms before men,
> to be seen of them, otherwise ye have no reward
> of your father which is in heaven. . . . When thou
> prayest, enter into thy closet, and when thou hast
> shut the door, pray to thy father which is in secret;
> and thy Father which seeth in secret shall reward
> thee openly." (Matt. vi. 1 & 6.)

I do not think that in any passage of the New Testament, the pursuit of fame is stated as a vice; it is only said that an action, to be virtuous, must be independent of it. I would also observe that it is not publicity, but ostentation, which is prohibited. A good man will prefer that mode, as well as those objects of his beneficence, by which he can produce the greatest effect; and the view of this purpose may dictate sometimes publication, and sometimes concealment. But from the motive, the reputation of the deed, and the fruits and advantage of that reputation to ourselves, must be shut out, or, in whatever proportion they are not so, the action in that proportion fails of being virtuous.

The true virtue is that which discards these considerations absolutely, and which retires from them all to the single internal purpose of pleasing God. This at least was the virtue which our Saviour taught. And in teaching this, he acted in consistency with his office as a monitor from heaven.

Next to what our Saviour taught, may be considered the manner of his teaching; which was precisely adapted to the peculiarity of his character and situation. His lessons did not consist of set treatises upon the several points which he mentioned. His instructions were conceived in short, emphatic, sententious rules, in occasional reflections, or in round maxims. He produced himself as a messenger from God. He put the truth of what he taught upon authority. In the choice of his mode of teaching, the purpose was impression: because conviction was to arise in the minds of his followers from their respect to his person and authority. Now, for the purpose of impression exclusively, I know nothing which would have so great force as strong ponderous maxims, frequently urged and frequently brought back to the thoughts of the hearers. I know nothing that could in this view be said better, than "Do unto others as ye would that others should do unto you:" "The first and great commandment is, Thou shalt love the Lord thy God: and the second is like unto it, Thou shalt love thy neighbour as thyself." It must also be remembered, that our Lord's ministry compared with his work, was of short duration; that, within this time, he had many places to visit, various audiences to address; that his person was generally besieged by crowds of followers; that he was, sometimes, driven away from the place where he was teaching by persecution. Under these circumstances, nothing appears to have been so practicable as leaving concise lessons of duty.

It is incidental to this mode of moral instruction, that the rules will be conceived in absolute terms, leaving the application and the distinctions that attend it to the reason of the hearer. It is further also that many of those strong instances which appear in our Lord's sermon, such as, "If any man will smite thee on the right cheek, turn to him the other also:" "If any man will sue thee at the law, and take away thy coat, let him have thy cloak also:" "Whosoever shall compel thee to go a mile, go with him twain:" though they appear in the form of specific precepts, are intended as descriptive of disposition and character.

One excellency of our Saviour's rules is, that they are never so mistaken as to do harm. I could feign a hundred cases in which the literal application of the rule, "of doing to others as we would that others should do unto us," might mislead us; but I never yet met with the man who was actually misled by it. Notwithstanding that our Lord bade his followers to "forgive the enemy who should trespass against them, not till seven times, but till seventy times seven," the Christian world has hitherto suffered little by too much placability or forbearance. These rules were designed to regulate personal conduct from personal motives, and for this purpose alone.

The parables of the New Testament are in the choice of the subjects, in the structure of the narratives, in the aptness, propriety, and force of the circumstances woven into them; and in some, as that of the Good Samaritan, the Prodigal Son, the Pharisee and the Publican, in an union of pathos and simplicity, the fruit only of a much exercised and well cultivated judgment.

The Lord's Prayer, for fixing the attention upon a few great points, for suitableness to every condition, for sufficiency, for conciseness without obscurity, for the weight and real importance of its petitions, is without an equal or a rival.

From whence did these come? Whence had this man his wisdom? Was our Saviour, in fact, a well instructed philosopher, whilst he is represented as an illiterate peasant? Or shall we say that some early Christians of education composed these pieces and ascribed them to Christ? No specimens of composition which the Christians of the first century have left us authorise us to believe that they were equal to the task. And how little qualified the Jews, the countrymen and companions of Christ, were to assist him, may be judged of from the writings of theirs which were the nearest to that age. The whole collection of the Talmud is proof of how little capable they were of furnishing out such lessons as Christ delivered.

But there is still another view in which our Lord's discourses deserve to be considered; and that is in what they did not contain. Under this head the following reflections appear to me to possess some weight.

I. They exhibit no particular description of the invisible world. The future happiness of the good, and the misery of the bad, which is all we want to be assured of, is directly and positively affirmed, and is represented by metaphors and comparisons, which were plainly intended as nothing more. As to the rest, a solemn reserve is maintained. I lay a stress upon this reserve, because it repels the suspicion of enthusiasm: for enthusiasm is wont to expatiate upon the condition of the departed, above all other subjects. It is moreover a topic which is always listened to with greediness. The Koran of Mahomet is half made up of it.

II. Our Lord enjoined no austerities. He not only enjoined none as absolute duties, but he recommended none as carrying men to a higher degree of Divine favour.

III. Our Saviour uttered no impassioned devotion. The Lord's Prayer is a model of calm devotion. His words in the garden are unaffected expressions of a deep, indeed, but sober piety.

IV. It is very usual with the human mind to substitute fervency in a particular cause for the merit of general and regular morality; and it is politic in the leader of a sect or party to encourage such a disposition in his followers. Christ did not overlook this turn of thought; yet, he notices it only to condemn it. "Not every one that saith unto me, Lord, Lord, shall enter into the kingdom of heaven; but he that doeth the will of my Father which is in heaven. Many will say unto me in that day, Lord, Lord, have we not prophesied in thy name? and in thy name have cast out devils? and in thy name done many wonderful works? And then will I profess unto you, I never knew you: depart from me, ye that work iniquity." (Matt. vii. 21, 22.) This was a proof both of sincerity and judgment.

V. Nor, fifthly, did he fall in with any of the depraved fashions of his country. Bred up a Jew, under a religion extremely technical, in an age and amongst a people more tenacious of the ceremonies than of any other part of that religion, he delivered an institution containing less of ritual than is to be found in any religion which ever prevailed. In both his treatment of the religion of his country and in the formation of his own institution, our Saviour displayed the soundness and moderation of his judgment. He censured an overstrained scrupulousness about the Sabbath: but how did he censure it? not by decrying the institution itself, but by declaring that "the Sabbath was made for man, not man for the Sabbath." This might be expected perhaps from a well-instructed and judicious philosopher, but was not to be looked for from an illiterate Jew.

VI. Nothing could be more quibbling than were the comments and expositions of the Jewish doctors at that time. Their evasion of the fifth commandment, their exposition of the law of oaths, are specimens of the bad taste in morals which then prevailed. Whereas, in a numerous collection of our Saviour's apophthegms, many of them referring to sundry precepts of the Jewish law, there is not to be found one example of sophistry.

VII. The national temper of the Jews was intolerant, narrow-minded, and excluding. In Jesus, we see benevolence the most enlarged and comprehensive. In the parable of the Good Samaritan, the very point of the story is, that the person relieved by him was the religious enemy of his benefactor. Our Lord declared the equity of the Divine administration, when he told the Jews, "That many should come from the east and west, and should sit down with Abraham, Isaac, and Jacob, in the kingdom of heaven; but that the children of the kingdom should be cast into outer darkness." (Matt. viii. 11.) His reproof of the hasty zeal of his disciples, who would needs call down fire from heaven to revenge an affront put upon their Master, shows the lenity of his character, and of his religion. The terms in which his rebuke was conveyed deserve to be noticed:—"Ye know not what manner of spirit ye are of." (Luke ix. 55.)

VIII. Lastly, amongst the negative qualities of our religion, as it came out of the hands of its Founder and his apostles, we may reckon its complete abstraction from all views either of ecclesiastical or civil policy. Christ's declaration, that "his kingdom was not of this world," recorded by Saint John; his evasion of the question, whether it was lawful or not to give tribute unto Caesar, mentioned by the three other evangelists; his reply to an application that was made to him, to interpose his authority in a question of property; "Man, who made me a ruler or a judge over you?" ascribed to him by St. Luke; his declining to exercise the office of a criminal judge in the case of the woman taken in adultery, as related by John, are all intelligible significations of our Saviour's sentiments upon this head. Had there been more to be found in Scripture of a political nature, or convertible to political purposes, the worst use would have been made of it, on whichever side it seemed to lie.

When, therefore, we consider Christ as a moral teacher; when we compare Christianity, as it came from its Author, with other religions, the most reluctant understanding will be induced to acknowledge the probity of those to whom it owes its origin; and that some regard is due to the testimony of such men, when they declare their knowledge that the religion proceeded from God.

Perhaps the qualities which we observe in the religion may prove something more. They would have been extraordinary had the religion come from any person; from the person from whom it did come, they are exceedingly so. What was Jesus in external appearance? A Jewish peasant, the son of a carpenter. He had no master to instruct or prompt him; he had read no books but the works of Moses and the prophets; he had visited no polished cities—nothing to form in him a taste or judgment different from that of the rest of his countrymen of the same rank of life with himself. Supposing it to be true, which it is not, that all his points of morality might be picked out of Greek and Roman writings, they were writings which he had never seen. Supposing them to be no more than what others had taught, he could not collect them together.

Who were his coadjutors in the undertaking? A few fishermen upon the lake of Tiberias, persons just as uneducated as himself. It is very difficult to explain how such a system should proceed from such persons.

The character of Christ is a part of the morality of the Gospel: he is never charged with any personal vice. This remark is as old as Origen: "Though innumerable lies and calumnies had been forged against the venerable Jesus, none had dared to charge him with an intemperance." (Or. Ep. Cels. 1. 3, num. 36, ed. Bened.) Not a reflection upon his moral character, not an imputation or suspicion of any offence against purity and chastity, appears for five hundred years after his birth. This faultlessness is more peculiar than we are apt to imagine. Some stain pollutes the morality of almost every other teacher, and of every other lawgiver.* One

---

* See many instances collected by Grotius, de Veritate Christianae Religionis, in the notes to his second book, p. 116. Pocock's edition.

loose principle is found in almost all the Pagan moralists. In speaking of the founders of new institutions we cannot forget Mahomet. His licentious transgressions of his own licentious rules is confessed by every writer of the Moslem story.

Secondly, in the histories which are left us of Jesus Christ we perceive traces of devotion, humility, benignity, mildness, patience, prudence. I speak of traces of these qualities, because the qualities themselves are to be collected from incidents; inasmuch as the terms are never used of Christ in the Gospels, nor is any formal character of him drawn in the New Testament.

Thus we see the devoutness of his mind in his frequent retirement to solitary prayer; (Matt. xiv. 23. Luke ix. 28. Matt. xxvi. 36.) in his habitual giving of thanks; (Matt. xi. 25. Mark viii. 6. John vi. 23. Luke xxii. 17.); in his reference of the beauties and operations of nature to the bounty of Providence; (Matt. vi, 26–28.) in his earnest addresses to his Father; ( John xi. 41.) and in the deep piety of his behaviour in the garden on the last evening of his life: (Matt. xxvi. 86–87.) his humility in his constant reproof of contentions for superiority: (Mark ix. 33.) the benignity and affectionateness of his temper in his kindness to children; (Mark x. 16.) in the tears which he shed over his falling country, (Luke xix. 41.) and upon the death of his friend; ( John xi. 35.) in his noticing of the widow's mite; (Mark xii. 42.) in his parables: the mildness and lenity of his character is discovered in his rebuke of the forward zeal of his disciples at the Samaritan village; (Luke ix. 55.) in his expostulation with Pilate; (John xix. 11.) in his prayer for his enemies at the moment of his suffering, (Luke xxiii. 34.) which was then new. His prudence is discerned in his conduct on trying occasions, and in answers to artful questions.

Our Saviour's lessons touch upon some of the most interesting topics of human duty, and of human meditation; upon the principles by which the decisions of the last day will be regulated; (Matt. xxv. 31, et seq.) upon the supreme importance of religion; ( Mark viii. 35. Matt. vi. 31–33. Luke xii. 4, 5, 16–21.) upon penitence; (Luke xv.) upon self-denial, (Matt. v. 29.) watchfulness, (Mark xiii. 37. Matt. xxiv. 42; xxv. 13.) placability, (Luke xvii. 4. Matt. xviii. 33, et seq.) confidence in God, (Matt. vi. 25–30.) the value of spiritual worship, (John iv. 23, 24.) the necessity of moral obedience, and the directing of that obedience to the spirit and principle of the law. (Matt. v. 21.)

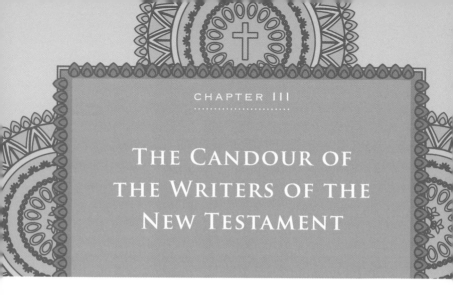

## CHAPTER III

# THE CANDOUR OF THE WRITERS OF THE NEW TESTAMENT

I make this candour to consist in their putting down many passages, which no writer was likely to have forged; and which no writer would have chosen who had thought himself at liberty to mould the particulars of that story according to his choice.

A strong example of the fairness of the evangelists offers itself in their account of Christ's resurrection, namely, in their unanimously stating that after he was risen he appeared to his disciples alone. The most common understanding must have perceived that the history of the resurrection would have come with more advantage if they had related that Jesus appeared, after he was risen, to his foes as well as his friends: or even if they had asserted the public appearance of Christ in general unqualified terms. And if they had thought of anything but of the truth of the case, as they believed it; they would in their account of Christ's several appearances after his resurrection, at least have omitted this restriction.

There are some other instances in which the evangelists honestly relate what they must have perceived would make against them.

Of this kind is John the Baptist's message preserved by Saint Matthew (xi. 2) and Saint Luke (vii. 18): "Now when John had heard in the prison the works of Christ, he sent two of his disciples, and said unto him, Art thou he that should come, or look we for another?" To confess that John the Baptist had his doubts concerning the character of Jesus, could not but afford a handle to objection. But truth neglects appearances. The same observation, perhaps, holds concerning the apostacy of Judas.

John vi. 66. "From that time, many of his disciples went back, and walked no more with him." Was it the part of a writer who dealt in suppression and disguise to put down this anecdote? Or this, which Matthew has preserved (xii. 58)? "He did not many mighty works there, because of their unbelief."

Again, in the same evangelist (v. 17, 18): "Think not that I am come to destroy the law or the prophets: I am not come to destroy, but to fulfil; for, verily, I say unto you, till heaven and earth pass, one jot, or one tittle, shall in no wise pass from the law, till all be fulfilled." At the time the Gospels were written, the apparent tendency of Christ's mission was to diminish the authority of the Mosaic code, and it was so considered by the Jews themselves. It is very improbable, therefore, that, without the constraint of truth, Matthew should have ascribed a saying to Christ, which, primo intuitu, militated with the judgment of the age in which his Gospel was written.

Lastly, where do we discern less disposition to extol and magnify, than in the conclusion of the same history? in which the evangelist, after relating that Paul, on his first arrival at Rome, preached to the Jews from morning until evening, adds, "And some believed the things which were spoken, and some believed not."

The following, I think, are passages which were very unlikely to have presented themselves to the mind of a forger or a fabulist.

Matt. xxi. 21. "Jesus answered and said unto them, Verily I say unto you, If ye have faith, and doubt not, ye shall not only do this which is done unto the fig-tree, but also, if ye shall say unto this mountain, Be thou removed, and be thou cast into the sea, it shall be done; all things whatsoever ye shall ask in prayer, believing, it shall be done." (See also chap. xvii. 20. Luke xvii. 6.) It appears to me very improbable that these words should have been put into Christ's mouth, if he had not actually spoken them. The words undoubtedly, in their obvious construction, carry with them a difficulty which no writer would have brought upon himself officiously.

Luke ix. 59. "And he said unto another, Follow me: but he said, Lord, suffer me first to go and bury my father. Jesus said unto him, Let the dead bury their dead, but go thou and preach the kingdom of God." (See also Matt. viii. 21.) This answer, though very expressive of the transcendent importance of religious concerns, was apparently harsh and repulsive; and such as would not have been made for Christ if he had not really used it.

The short reply of our Lord to Mary Magdalen, after his resurrection (John xx. 16, 17), "Touch me not, for I am not yet ascended unto my Father," in my opinion must have been founded in a reference or allusion to some prior conversation, for the want of knowing which his meaning is hidden from us. This very obscurity, however, is a proof of genuineness. No one would have forged such an answer.

John vi. The whole of the conversation recorded in this chapter is in the highest degree unlikely to be fabricated, especially the part of our Saviour's reply between the fiftieth and the fifty-eighth verse. I need only put down the first sentence: "I am the living bread which came down from heaven: if any man eat of this bread he shall live for ever: and the bread that I will give him is my flesh, which I will give for the life of the world." Without calling in question the expositions that have been given of this passage, we may be permitted to say, that it labours under an obscurity, in which it is impossible to believe that any one would have voluntarily involved them. That this discourse was obscure, even at the time, is confessed by the writer who had preserved it.

Christ's taking of a young child, and placing it in the midst of his contentious disciples (Matt. xviii. 2), though very expressive of the character of the religion which he wished to inculcate, was not by any means an obvious thought.

The account of the institution of the eucharist bears strong internal marks of genuineness. If it had been feigned, it would have come nearer to the actual mode of celebrating the rite as that mode obtained very early in the Christian churches; and it would have been more formal than it is. Whereas, as we read it in Saint Matthew's Gospel, there is not so much as the command to repeat it. This, surely, looks like undesignedness. I think also that the difficulty arising from the conciseness of Christ's expression, "This is my body," would have been avoided in a made-up story.

The argument which is built upon these examples extends both to the authenticity of the books, and to the truth of the narrative; for it is improbable that the forger of a history in the name of another should have inserted such passages into it: and it is improbable, also, that the persons whose names the books bear should have fabricated such passages; or even have allowed them a place in their work, if they had not believed them to express the truth.

## CHAPTER IV

# IDENTITY OF CHRIST'S
# CHARACTER

The argument expressed by this title I apply principally
to the comparison of the first three Gospels with that
of Saint John. The passages of Christ's history preserved by
Saint John are, except his passion and resurrection, different from those which are delivered by the other evangelists.
And I think the ancient account of this difference to be
that Saint John wrote after the rest, and to supply what he
thought omissions in their narratives. Under this diversity,
there is a similitude of manner, which indicates that the
actions and discourses proceeded from the same person. I
should have laid little stress upon the repetition of actions
substantially alike, or of discourses containing many of the
same expressions, because that resemblance would either
belong to a true history, or be imitate in a false one. Nor do
I deny that a dramatic writer is able to sustain distinction
of character through a great variety of situations. But the

evangelists were not dramatic writers; nor will it be suspected that they studied uniformity of character. Such uniformity, if it exist, is on their part casual; and if there be a perceptible resemblance of manner, in passages, and between discourses, which are in themselves extremely distinct, and are delivered by historians writing without any reference to one another, it affords a just presumption that these are the actions and the discourses of the same real person.

The article in which I find this agreement most strong is in our Saviour's mode of teaching.

It will be my business to point out this manner in the first three evangelists; and then to inquire whether it do not appear also in several examples of Christ's discourses preserved by Saint John.

Matt. xii. 47–50. "Then they said unto him, Behold, thy mother and thy brethren stand without, desiring to speak with thee. But he answered and said unto him that told him, Who is my mother; and who are my brethren? And he stretched forth his hand towards his disciples, and said, Behold my mother and my brethren: for whosoever shall do the will of my Father which is in heaven, the same is my brother, and sister, and mother."

Matt. xv. 1, 2; 10, 11; 15–20. "Then came to Jesus scribes and Pharisees, which were of Jerusalem, saying, Why do thy disciples transgress the traditions of the elders? for they wash not their hands when they eat bread.—And he called the multitude, and said unto them, Hear and understand: Not that which goeth into the mouth defileth a man, but that which cometh out of the mouth, this defileth the man.—Then answered Peter, and said unto him, Declare unto us this parable. And Jesus said, Are ye also yet without understanding? Do ye not understand that whatsoever entereth in at the mouth goeth into the belly, and is cast out into the draught? but those things which proceed out of the mouth come forth from the heart, and they defile the man: for out of the heart proceed evil thoughts, murders, adulteries, fornications, thefts, false witness, blasphemies; these are the things which defile a man: *but to eat with unwashen hands defileth not a man.*"

Mark x. 13, 14, 15. "And they brought young children to him, that he should touch them; and his disciples rebuked those that brought them: but when Jesus saw it, he was much displeased, and said unto them, Suffer the little children to come unto me, and forbid them not; for of such is the kingdom of God: verily I say unto you, whosoever shall not receive the kingdom of God as a little child, he shall not enter therein."

Mark i. 16, 17. "Now as he walked by the sea of Galilee, he saw Simon and Andrew his brother casting a net into the sea, for they were fishers: and Jesus said unto them, Come ye after me, and I will make you fishers of men."

Luke xi. 27. "And it came to pass as he spake these things, a certain woman of the company lifted up her voice, and said unto him, Blessed is the womb that bare thee, and the paps which thou hast sucked: but he said, Yea, rather, blessed are they that hear the word of God and keep it."

Luke xiii. 1–3. "There were present at that season some that told him of the Galileans, whose blood Pilate had mingled with their sacrifices; and Jesus answering said unto them, Suppose ye, that these Galileans were sinners above all the Galileans, because they suffered such things? I tell you, Nay: but, except ye repent, ye shall all likewise perish."

We will now see how this manner discovers itself in Saint John's history of Christ.

John vi. 25. "And when they had found him on the other side of the sea, they said unto him, Rabbi, when camest thou hither? Jesus answered them and said, Verily I say unto you, ye seek me not because ye saw the miracles, but because ye did eat of the loaves and were filled. Labour not for the meat which perisheth, but for that meat which endureth unto everlasting life, which the Son of man shall give unto you."

John iv. 12. "Art thou greater than our father Abraham, who gave us the well, and drank thereof himself, and his children, and his cattle? Jesus answered, and said unto her (the woman of Samaria), Whosoever drinketh of this water shall thirst again; but whosoever drinketh of the water that I shall give him, shall never thirst; but the water that I shall give him shall be in him a well of water, springing up into everlasting life."

John ix. 1–5. "And as Jesus passed by, he saw a man which was blind from his birth: and his disciples asked him, saying, Who did sin, this man or his parents, that he was born blind? Jesus answered, Neither hath this man sinned, nor his parents, but that the works of God should be made manifest in him. I must work the works of Him that sent me while it is day; the night cometh when no man can work. As long as I am in the world, I am the light of the world."

Compare the series of examples taken from Saint John with the series of examples taken from the other evangelists, and judge whether there be not a visible agreement of manner between them.

I conclude this article by remarking, that nothing of this manner is perceptible in any other speeches but those which are attributed to Christ. A forger would have made for Christ, discourses exhorting to virtue and dissuading from vice in general terms. It would never have entered into his thoughts to have crowded together such a number of allusions to time, place, and other little circumstances, as occur, for instance, in the sermon on the mount, and which nothing but the actual presence of the objects could have suggested (See Bishop Law's *Life of Christ*).

II. There appears to me to exist an affinity between the history of Christ's placing a little child in the midst of his disciples, as related by the first three evangelists, (Matt. xviii. 1. Mark ix. 33. Luke ix. 46.) and the history of Christ's washing his disciples' feet, as given by Saint John. (Chap. xiii. 3.) The affinity consists in these two articles: First, that both stories denote the emulation which prevailed amongst Christ's disciples, and his own care and desire to correct it.

Secondly, that both stories are specimens of teaching by action; a mode of emblematic instruction ascribed to our Saviour by the first three evangelists, and by Saint John, in instances totally unlike.

III. A singularity in Christ's language which runs through all the evangelists, and which is found in those discourses of Saint John, is the appellation of "the Son of man;" and it is in all the evangelists found under the peculiar circumstance of being applied by Christ to himself, but of never being used of him, or towards him, by any other person. It occurs seventeen times in Matthew's Gospel, twenty times in Mark's, twenty-one times in Luke's and eleven times in John's, and always with this restriction.

IV. A point of agreement in the conduct of Christ is that of his withdrawing himself out of the way whenever the behaviour of the multitude indicated a disposition to tumult.

Matt. xiv. 22. "And straightway Jesus constrained his disciples to get into a ship, and to go before him unto the other side, while he sent the multitude away. And when he had sent the multitude away, he went up into a mountain apart to pray."

Luke v. 15, 16. "But so much the more went there a fame abroad of him, and great multitudes came together to hear, and to be healed by him of their infirmities; and he withdrew himself into the wilderness and prayed." With these quotations compare the following from Saint John:

Chap. v. 13. "And he that was healed wist not who it was, for Jesus had conveyed himself away, a multitude being in that place."

Chap. vi. 15. "When Jesus therefore perceived that they would come and take him by force, to make him a king, he departed again into a mountain himself alone."

In this last instance, Saint John gives the motive of Christ's conduct, which is left unexplained by the other evangelists.

V. Another more singular circumstance in Christ's ministry, was the reserve which he used in declaring his own character. Just reasons for this reserve have been assigned. (See Locke's Reasonableness of Christianity.) But it is not what one would have expected. We meet with it in Saint Matthew's Gospel (chap. xvi. 20): "Then charged he his disciples that they should tell no man that he was Jesus the Christ." Again, and upon a different occasion, in Saint Mark's (chap. iii. 11): "And unclean spirits, when they saw him, fell down before him, and cried, saying, Thou art the Son of God: and he straitly charged them that they should not make him known." Another is recorded by Saint Luke (chap. iv. 41). What we thus find in the three evangelists, appears also in a passage of Saint John (chap. x. 24, 25): "Then came the Jews round about him, and said unto him, How long dost thou make us to doubt: If thou be the Christ, tell us plainly." The occasion here was different from any of the rest; and it was indirect. We only discover

Christ's conduct through the upbraidings of his adversaries. But all this strengthens the argument.

VI. In our Lord's commerce with his disciples, one particular is the difficulty which they found in understanding him when he spoke to them of the future part of his history. This difficulty produced a wish in them to ask for further explanation: from which, however, they appear to have been kept back by the fear of giving offence. All these circumstances are noticed by Mark and Luke, upon the occasion of his informing them that the Son of man should be delivered into the hands of men. "They understood not," the evangelists tell us, "this saying, and it was hid from them, that they perceived it not; and they feared to ask him of that saying." Luke ix. 45; Mark ix. 32. In Saint John's Gospel we have, on a different occasion, the same difficulty and restraint:— "A little while and ye shall not see me; and again, a little while and ye shall see me, because I go to the Father. Then said some of his disciples among themselves, What is this that he saith unto us? A little while and ye shall not see me: and again, a little while and ye shall see me: and, Because I go to the Father? They said, therefore, What is this that he saith? A little while? We cannot tell what he saith. Now Jesus knew that they were desirous to ask him, and said unto them,—" &c. John xvi. 16, et seq.

VII. The meekness of Christ during his last sufferings, which is conspicuous in the narratives of the first three evangelists, is preserved in that of Saint John. The answer given by him, in Saint John, (Chap. xviii. 20, 21.) when the high priest asked him of his doctrine; "I spake openly to the world: I ever taught in the synagogue, and in the temple, whither the Jews always resort; and in secret have I said nothing. Why askest thou me? ask them which heard me what I have said unto them," is very much of a piece with his reply to the armed party which seized him, as we read it in Saint Mark's Gospel, and in Saint Luke's: (Mark xiv. 48. Luke xxii. 52.) "Are you come out as against a thief, with swords and with staves to take me? I was daily with you in the temple teaching, and ye took me not." In both answers we discern the same tranquillity, the same reference to his public teaching. His mild expostulation with Pilate, on two several occasions, as related by Saint John, (Chap. xviii. 34; xix. 11.) is delivered with the same unruffled temper. His answer, in Saint John's Gospel, to the officer who struck him with the palm of his hand, "If I have spoken evil, bear witness of the evil; but if well, why smitest thou me?" (Chap. xviii. 23.) was such an answer as might have been looked for from the person who, as he proceeded to the place of execution, bid his companions ( Luke; Chap. xxiii. 28.) weep not for him, but for themselves, their posterity, and their country; and who, whilst he was suspended upon the cross, prayed for his murderers, "for they know not," said he, "what they do." The urgency also of his prosecutors to extort from him a defence to the accusation, and his unwillingness to make any, appears in Saint John's account, as well as in that of the other evangelists. (See John xix. 9. Matt. xxvii. 14. Luke xxiii. 9.)

There are, moreover, two other correspondencies between Saint John's history of the transaction and theirs.

The first three evangelists record our Saviour's devotion in the garden immediately before he was apprehended; in which narrative they all make him pray "that the cup might pass from him." This is the particular metaphor which they all ascribe to him. Now Saint John does not give the scene in the garden: but when Jesus was seized, and some resistance was attempted to be made by Peter, Jesus checked the attempt, with this reply: "Put up thy sword into the sheath; the cup which my Father hath given me, shall I not drink it?" (Chap. xviii. 11.) It is extremely natural that Jesus, who had been praying his Father that "that cup might pass from him," yet with such a pious retraction of his request as to have added, "If this cup may not pass from me, thy will be done;" it was natural, I say, when he actually was apprehended, to express the resignation in the form of speech which he had before used, "The cup which my Father hath given me, shall I not drink it?" This is a coincidence between writers in whose narratives there is no imitation, but great diversity.

A second similar correspondency is the following: Matthew and Mark make the charge upon which our Lord was condemned to be a threat of destroying the temple; "We heard him say, I will destroy this temple made with hands, and within three days I will build another made without hands:" (Mark xiv. 58.) but they neither of them inform us upon what circumstance this calumny was founded. Saint John (Chap. ii. 19.) supplies us with this information; for he relates, that on our Lord's first journey to Jerusalem, when the Jews asked him "What sign showest thou unto us, seeing that thou doest these things? He answered, Destroy this temple, and in three days I will raise it up." This agreement could hardly arise from anything but the truth of the case.

A strong and more general instance of agreement is the following.—The first three evangelists have related the appointment of the twelve apostles; (Matt. x. 1. Mark iii. 14. Luke vi. 12.). John, without ever mentioning the appointment, supposes, throughout his whole narrative, Christ to be accompanied by a select party of disciples; the number of these to be twelve; (Chap. vi. 70.) and whenever he happens to notice any one as of that number, (Chap. xx, 24; vi. 71.) it is one included in the catalogue of the other evangelists. This last agreement runs through every Gospel, and through every chapter of each. All this bespeaks reality.

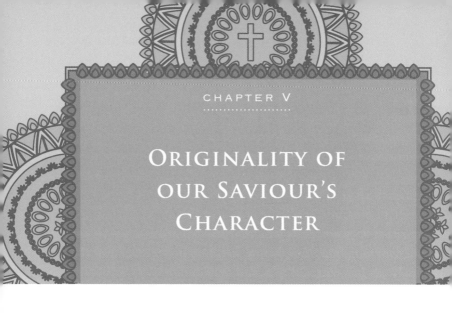

## CHAPTER V

# ORIGINALITY OF OUR SAVIOUR'S CHARACTER

The Jews had understood their prophecies to foretell the advent of a person who by some supernatural assistance should advance their nation to independence. Now, had Jesus been an enthusiast, it is probable that his enthusiasm would have fallen in with the popular delusion, and that, while he gave himself out to be the person intended by these predictions, he would have assumed the character to which they were supposed to relate.

But what is better than conjectures is the fact, that all the pretended Messiahs actually did so. We learn from Josephus that there were many of these. But whether impostors or enthusiasts, they concurred in producing themselves as the restorers and deliverers of the nation, in that sense in which restoration and deliverance were expected by the Jews.

Why therefore Jesus, if he was either an enthusiast or impostor, did not pursue the same conduct, it will be difficult to explain. A mission, the operation and benefit of which was to take place in another life, was a thing unthought of as the subject of these prophecies. That Jesus, coming to them as their Messiah, should deviate from the general persuasion into pretensions absolutely singular and original—appears to be inconsistent with the imputation of enthusiasm or imposture.

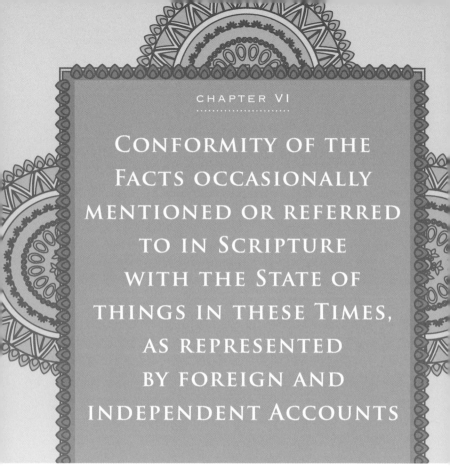

# CONFORMITY OF THE FACTS OCCASIONALLY MENTIONED OR REFERRED TO IN SCRIPTURE WITH THE STATE OF THINGS IN THESE TIMES, AS REPRESENTED BY FOREIGN AND INDEPENDENT ACCOUNTS

One argument which has been much relied upon is the conformity of the facts referred to in Scripture with the state of things in those times, as represented by foreign and independent accounts; which proves, that the writers of the New Testament possessed local knowledge which could belong only to an inhabitant of that country living in that age. This is very little short of proving the genuineness of the writings. It carries them up to the age of the reputed authors, an age in which it must have been difficult to impose upon the Christian public forgeries in the names of those authors. It proves that the books were composed by persons living in the time and country in which these things were transacted; and consequently capable of being well informed of the facts which they relate. And the argument is stronger when applied to the New Testament, by reason of the mixed nature of the allusions which this book contains. The scene of action is not confined to a single country, but displayed in the greatest cities of the Roman empire. Allusions are made to the manners and principles of the Greeks, the Romans, and the Jews. This variety renders a forgery proportionably more difficult, especially to writers of a posterior age. (Michaelis's Introduction to the New Testament [Marsh's translation], c. ii. sect. xi.)

This is an argument which depends entirely upon an induction of particulars; I have a detail of examples, distinctly and articulately proposed. In collecting these examples I have done no more than epitomise the first volume of the first part of Dr. Lardner's Credibility of the Gospel History.

The writer principally made use of in the inquiry is Josephus. Josephus was born at Jerusalem four years after Christ's ascension. He wrote his history some time after the destruction of Jerusalem, which happened thirty-seven years after the ascension; and his history of the Jews he finished sixty years after the ascension. At the head of each article I have referred, by figures included in brackets, to the page of Dr. Lardner's volume where the section begins. The edition used is that of 1741.

I. [p. 14.] Matt. ii. 22. "When he (Joseph) heard that Archclaus did reign in Judea in the room of his father Herod, he was afraid to go thither: notwithstanding, being warned of God in a dream, he turned aside into the parts of Galilee."

In this passage it is asserted that Archclaus succeeded Herod in Judea; and it is implied that his power did not extend to Galilee.

Agreeably, we are informed by Josephus, that Herod appointed Archclaus his successor in Judea with the title of King; and the Greek verb basileuei, which the evangelist uses to denote the rank of Archclaus, is used likewise by Josephus (De Bell. lib. i. c. 3,3, sect. 7.).

The cruelty of Archelaus's character, which is intimated by the evangelist, agrees with his history preserved by Josephus:—"In the tenth year of his government, the chief of the Jews and Samaritans, not being able to endure his cruelty and tyranny, presented complaints against him to Caesar." (Ant, lib. xii. 13, sect. 1.)

II. [p. 19.] Luke iii. 1. "In the fifteenth year of the reign of Tiberius Caesar—Herod being tetrarch of Galilee, and his brother Philip tetrarch of Iturea, and of the region of Trachonitis—the word of God came unto John."

By the will of Herod the Great, his two sons were appointed, one (Herod Antipus) tetrarch of Galilee and Peraea, and the other (Philip) tetrarch of Trachonitis and the neighbouring countries. (Ant. lib. xvii. c. 8, sect. 1.) We have these two persons in the situations in which Saint Luke places them; and also, in these situations in the fifteenth year of Tiberius and afterwards, appears from a passage of Josephus, which relates of Herod, "that he was removed by Caligula, the successor of Tiberius;" (Ant. lib. xviii. c. 8, sect. 2.) and of Philip, that he died in the twentieth year of Tiberius. (Ant. lib. xviii. c. 5, sect. 6.)

III. [p. 20.] Mark vi. 17. "Herod had sent forth, and laid hold upon John, and bound him in prison, for Herodias' sake, his brother Philip's wife: for he had married her." (See also Matt. xiv. 1–13; Luke iii. 19.)

With this compare Joseph. Antiq. 1. xviii. c. 6, sect. 1:—"He (Herod the tetrarch) made a visit to Herod his brother.—Here, falling in love with Herodias, the wife of the said Herod, he ventured to make her proposals of marriage."*

With this also compare Joseph. Antiq. 1. xviii. c. 6, sect. 4. "Herodias was married to Herod, son of Herod the Great.

---

* The affinity of the two accounts is unquestionable; but there is a difference in the name of Herodias's first husband, which in the evangelist is Philip; in Josephus, Herod. The difficulty, however, will not appear considerable when we recollect how common it was in those times for the same persons to bear two names. Lardner, vol. ii. p. 897.

They had a daughter, whose name was Salome; after whose birth Herodias, in utter violation of the laws of her country, left her husband, then living, and married Herod the tetrarch of Galilee, her husband's brother by the father's side."

IV. [p. 29.] Acts xii. 1. "Now, about that time, Herod the king stretched forth his hands, to vex certain of the church."

In the conclusion of the same chapter, Herod's death is represented to have taken place soon after this persecution. There was no portion of time for thirty years before, nor ever afterwards, in which there was a king at Jerusalem, a person exercising that authority in Judea, or to whom that title could be applied, except the last three years of this Herod's life, within which period the transaction recorded in the Acts is stated to have taken place. This prince was the grandson of Herod the Great. In the Acts he appears under his family-name of Herod; by Josephus he was called Agrippa. For proof that he was a king we have the testimony of Josephus:—"Sending for him to his palace, Caligula put a crown upon his head, and appointed him king of the tetrarchie of Philip, intending also to give him the tetrarchie of Lysanias." (Antiq. xviii. c. 7, sect. 10.) And that Judea was at last included in his dominions, appears by a subsequent passage of the same Josephus, wherein he tells us that Claudius confirmed to Agrippa the dominion which Caligula had given him; adding also Judea and Samaria, as possessed by his grandfather Herod (Antiq. xix. c. 5, sect. 1.).

V. [p. 32.] Acts xii. 19–23. "And he (Herod) went down from Judea to Cesarea, and there abode. And on a set day Herod, arrayed in royal apparel, sat upon his throne, and made an oration unto them: and the people gave a shout, saying, It is the voice of a god, and not of a man; and immediately the angel of the Lord smote him, because he gave *not God the glory: and he was eaten of worms, and gave up the ghost.*"

Joseph. Antiq. lib. xix. c. 8, sect. 2. "He went to the city of Cesarea. Here he celebrated shows in honour of Caesar. On the second day of the shows, early in the morning, he came into the theatre, dressed in a robe of silver, of most curious workmanship. The rays of the rising sun, reflected from such a splendid garb, gave him a majestic and awful appearance. They called him a god; and intreated him to be propitious to them, saying, Hitherto we have respected you as a man; but now we acknowledge you to be more than mortal. The king neither reproved these persons, nor rejected the impious flattery. Immediately after this he was seized with pains in his bowels, extremely violent at the very first. He was carried therefore with all haste to his palace. These pains continually tormenting him, he expired in five days' time."

The reader will perceive the accordancy of these accounts in various particulars.

VI. [p. 41.] Acts xxiv. 24. "And after certain days, when Felix came with his wife Drusilla, which was a Jewess, he sent for Paul."

Joseph. Antiq. lib. xx. c. 6, sect. 1, 2. "Agrippa gave his sister Drusilla in marriage to Azizus, king of the Emesenes, when he had consented to be circumcised.—But this marriage of Drusilla with Azizus was dissolved in a short time after, in this manner:—When Felix was procurator of Judea, having had a sight of her, he was mightily taken with her.— She was induced to transgress the laws of her country, and marry Felix."

Here the public station of Felix, the name of his wife, and the singular circumstance of her religion, all appear in perfect conformity with the evangelist.

VII. [p. 46.] Acts xxv. 13. "And after certain days king Agrippa and Berenice came to Cesarea to salute Festus." By this passage we are told that Agrippa was a king, but not of Judea; for he came to salute Festus, who at this time administered the government of that country at Cesarea.

The Agrippa here spoken of was the son of Herod Agrippa; but that he did not succeed to his father's kingdom, nor ever recovered Judea, we learn by the information of Josephus, who relates of him that when his father was dead Claudius intended to have put him immediately in possession of his father's dominions; but that, Agrippa being then but seventeen years of age, the emperor was persuaded to alter his mind, and appointed Cuspius Fadus prefect of Judea and the whole kingdom; (Antiq. xi. c. 9 ad fin.) which Fadus was succeeded by Tiberius Alexander, Cumanus, Felix, Festus. (Antiq. xx. de Bell. lib. ii.) But that, he was rightly styled King Agrippa, and that he was in possession of considerable territories, bordering upon Judea, we gather from the same authority: for, after several successive donations of country, "Claudius, at the same time that he sent Felix to be procurator of Judea, promoted Agrippa from Chalcis to a greater kingdom, giving to him the tetrarchie which had been Philip's; and he added, moreover, the kingdom of Lysanias, and the province that had belonged to Varus." (De Bell. lib. li. c. 12 ad fin.)

Saint Paul addresses this person as a Jew: "King Agrippa, believest thou the prophets? I know that thou believest." As the son of Herod Agrippa, a zealous Jew, it is reasonable to suppose that he maintained the same profession. But what is more material to remark, is, that Saint Luke, speaking of the father (Acts xii. 1–3), calls him Herod the king, and gives an example of the exercise of his authority at Jerusalem: speaking of the son (xxv. 13), he calls him king, but not of Judea; which distinction agrees correctly with the history.

VIII. [p. 51.] Acts xiii. 6. "And when they had gone through the isle (Cyprus) to Paphos, they found a false prophet, a Jew, whose name was Bar-jesus, which was with the deputy of the country, Sergius Paulus, a prudent man."

The word which is here translated deputy, signifies and upon this word our observation is founded. The provinces of the Roman empire were of two kinds; those belonging to the emperor, in which the governor was called proprietor; those belonging to the senate, in which the governor was proconsul. Now it appears from Dio Cassius, (Lib. liv. ad A. U. 732.) that the province of Cyprus, which, had transferred to the senate, the appropriate title of the Roman was proconsul.

Ib. xviii. 12. [p. 55.] "And when Gallio was deputy (proconsul) of Achaia."

The propriety of the title "proconsul" is in this still more critical. For the province of Achaia, had been restored by the emperor Claudius to the senate only six or seven years before the time in which this transaction is said to have taken place. (Suet. in Claud. c. xxv. Dio, lib. lxi.) And what confines with strictness the appellation to the time is, that Achaia under the following reign ceased to be a Roman province at all.

IX. [p. 152.] It appears, from what Josephus delivers concerning the state of Judea in particular, (Antiq. lib. xx. c. 8, sect. 5; c. 1, sect. 2.) that the power of life and death resided exclusively in the Roman governor; but that the Jews had magistrates and a council, invested with a subordinate and municipal authority. This economy is discerned in every part of the Gospel narrative of our Saviour's crucifixion.

X. [p. 203.] Acts ix. 31. "Then had the churches rest throughout all Judea and Galilee and Samaria."

This rest synchronises with the attempt of Caligula to place his statue in the temple of Jerusalem; the threat of which outrage produced amongst the Jews a consternation that, for a season, diverted their attention from every other object. (Joseph. de Bell lib. Xi. c. 13, sect. 1, 3, 4.)

XI. [p. 218.] Acts xxi. 30. "And they took Paul, and drew him out of the temple; and forthwith the doors were shut. And as they went about to kill him, tidings came to the chief captain of the band that all Jerusalem was in an uproar. Then the chief captain came near, and took him and commanded him to be bound with two chains, and demanded who he was, and what he had done; and some cried one thing, and some another, among the multitude: and, when he could not know the certainty for the tumult, he commanded him to be carried into the castle. And when he came upon the stairs, so it was, that he was borne of the soldiers for the violence of the people."

In this quotation we have the band of Roman soldiers at Jerusalem, the castle, the stairs, both adjoining to the temple.

Joseph. de. Bell. lib. v. e. 5, sect. 8. "Antonia was situated at the angle of the western and northern porticoes of the outer temple. It was built upon a rock fifty cubits high, steep on all sides.—On that side where it joined to the porticoes of the temple, there were stairs reaching to each portico, by which the guard descended; for there was always lodged here a Roman legion; and posting themselves in their armour in several places in the porticoes, they kept a watch on the people on the feast-days to prevent all disorders; for as the temple was a guard to the city, so was Antonia to the temple."

XII. [p. 224.] Acts iv. 1. "And as they spake unto the people, the priests, and the captain of the temple, and the Sadducees, came upon them." Here we have a public officer, under the title of captain of the temple, and he probably a Jew.

Joseph. de Bell. lib. ii. c. 17, sect. 2. "And at the temple, Eleazer, the son of Ananias the high priest, a young man of a bold and resolute disposition, then captain, persuaded those who performed the sacred ministrations not to receive the gift or sacrifice of any stranger."

XIII. [p. 225.] Acts xxv. 12. "Then Festus, when he had conferred with the council, answered, Hast thou appealed unto Caesar? unto Caesar shalt thou go." That it was usual for the Roman presidents to have a council appears expressly in the following passage of Cicero's oration against Verres:—"Illud negare posses, aut nunc negabis, te, concilio tuo dimisso, viris primariis, qui in consilio C. Sacerdotis fuerant, tibique esse volebant, remotis, de re judicata judicasse?"

XIV. [p. 235.] Acts xvi. 13. "And (at Philippi) on the Sabbath we went out of the city by a river-side, where prayer was wont to be made," or where a place of prayer was allowed. The particularity to be remarked is, the situation of the place where prayer was wont to be made, viz. by a river-side.

Philo, describing the conduct of the Jews of Alexandria relates of them, that, "early in the morning, flocking out of the gates of the city, they go to the neighbouring shores, (for the proseuchai were destroyed,) and, standing in a most pure place, they lift up their voices with one accord." (Philo in Flacc. p. 382.)

Josephus gives us a decree of the city of Halicarnassus, permitting the Jews to build oratories; a part of which decree runs thus:—"We ordain that the Jews, who are willing, men and women, do observe the Sabbaths, and perform sacred rites, according to the Jewish laws, and build oratories by the sea-side." (Joseph. Antiq. lib. xiv. c. 10, sect, 24.)

XV. [p. 255.] Acts xxvi. 5. "After the most straitest sect of our religion, I lived a Pharisee."

Joseph. de Bell. lib. i. c. 5, sect. 2. "The Pharisees were reckoned the most religious of any of the Jews, and to be the most exact and skilful in explaining the laws."

XVI. [p. 255.] Mark vii. 3,4. "The Pharisees and all the Jews, except they wash, eat not, holding the tradition of the elders; and many other things there be which they have received to hold."

Joseph. Antiq. lib. xiii. c. 10, sect. 6. "The Pharisees have delivered up to the people many institutions, as received from the fathers, which are not written in the law of Moses."

XVII. [p. 259.] Acts xxiii. 8. "For the Sadducees say, that there is no resurrection, neither angel, nor spirit; but the Pharisees confess both."

Joseph. de Bell. lib. ii. c. 8, sect. 14. "They (the Pharisees) bclieve every soul to be immortal, but that the soul of the good only passes into another body, and that the soul of the wicked is punished with eternal punishment." On the other hand (Antiq. lib. xviii. e. 1, sect. 4), "It is the opinion of the Sadducees that souls perish with the bodies."

XVIII. [p. 268.] Acts v. 17. "Then the high priest rose up, and all they that were with him (which is the sect of the Sadducees), and were filled with indignation." Saint Luke here intimates that the high priest was a Sadducee; which is a character one would not have expected to meet with in that station. This circumstance, remarkable as it is, was not however without examples.

Joseph. Antiq. lib. xiii. c. 10, sect. 6, 7. "John Hyreanus, high priest of the Jews, forsook the Pharisees upon a disgust, and joined himself to the party of the Sadducees." This high priest died one hundred and seven years before the Christian era.

Again (Antiq. lib. xx. e. 8, sect. 1), "This Ananus the younger, who, as we have said just now, had received the high priesthood, was fierce and haughty in his behaviour, and, above all men, bold and daring, and, moreover, was of the sect of the Sadducees." This high priest lived little more than twenty years after the transaction in the Acts.

XIX. [p. 282.] Luke ix. 51. "And it came to pass, when the time was come that he should be received up, he steadfastly set his face to go to Jerusalem, and sent messengers before his face.

And they went, and entered into a village of the Samaritans, to make ready for him. And they did not receive him, because his face was as though he would go to Jerusalem."

Joseph. Antiq. lib. xx. c. 5, sect. 1. "It was the custom of the Galileans, who went up to the holy city at the feasts, to travel through the country of Samaria. As they were in their journey, some inhabitants of the village called Ginaea, which lies on the borders of Samaria and the great plain, falling upon them, killed a great many of them."

XX. [p. 278.] John iv. 20. "Our fathers," said the Samaritan woman, "worshipped in this mountain; and ye say, that Jerusalem is the place where men ought to worship."

Joseph. Antiq. lib. xviii. c. 5, sect. 1. "Commanding them to meet him at mount Gerizzim, which is by them (the Samaritans) esteemed the most sacred of all mountains."

The examples here collected will be sufficient, I hope, to satisfy us that the writers of the Christian history knew something of what they were writing about. The argument is also strengthened by the following considerations:

I. That these agreements appear not only in articles of public history, but sometimes in very peculiar circumstances, in which a forger is most likely to have been found tripping.

II. That the destruction of Jerusalem, which took place forty years after the commencement of the

Christian institution, produced such a change in the condition of the Jews, that a writer who was unacquainted with the circumstances of the nation before that event would find it difficult to avoid mistakes, in endeavouring to give detailed accounts of transactions connected with those circumstances.

III. That there appears, in the writers of the New Testament, a knowledge of the affairs of those times which we do not find in authors of later ages. In particular, "many of the Christian writers of the second and third centuries, and of the following ages, had false notions concerning the state of Judea between the nativity of Jesus and the destruction of Jerusalem." (Lardner, part i. vol. ii. p. 960.) Therefore they could not have composed our histories.

Amidst so many conformities we meet with some difficulties. The principal of these I will put down, together with the solutions which they have received. For the historical proofs of my assertions I refer the reader to the second volume of the first part of Dr. Lardner's large work.

I. The taxing during which Jesus was born was "first made," as we read, according to our translation, in Saint Luke, "whilst Cyrenius was governor of Syria." (Chap. ii. ver. 2.) Now it turns out that Cyrenius was not governor of Syria until twelve, or ten years after the birth of Christ; and that a taxing census was made in Judea, in the beginning of his government. The charge brought against the evangelist is, that, intending to refer to this taxing, he has misplaced the date of it.

The answer to the accusation is founded in his using the word "first:"— "And this taxing was first made:" for, according to the mistake imputed to the evangelist, this word could have no signification whatever; because, let it relate to what taxing, census, enrolment, or assessment, it imports that the writer had more than one of those in contemplation. It acquits him therefore of the charge: it is inconsistent with the supposition of his knowing only of the taxing in the beginning of Cyrenius's government. And if the evangelist knew of some other taxing beside that, it is too much to lay it down as certain that he intended to refer to that.

The sentence in Saint Luke may be construed thus: "This was the first assessment (or enrolment) of Cyrenius, governor of Syria;"* the words "governor of Syria" being used after the name of Cyrenius as his addition or title. And this title, belonging to him at the time of writing the account, was naturally enough subjoined to his name, though acquired after the transaction which the account

---

* If the word which we render "first" be rendered "before," which it has been strongly contended that the Greek idiom shows of, the whole difficulty vanishes: for then the passage would be,—"Now this taxing was made before Cyreulus was governor of Syria;" which corresponds with the chronology.

describes. And this, as we contend, is precisely the inaccuracy which has produced the difficulty in Saint Luke.

It appears from the form of the expression that he had two taxings or enrolments in contemplation. And if Cyrenius had been sent upon this business into Judea before he became governor of Syria (there is external evidence of an enrolment going on about this time under some person or other*), then the census on all hands acknowledged to have been made by him in the beginning of his government would form a second, so as to occasion the other to be called the first.

II. Another chronological objection arises upon a date assigned in the the third chapter of Saint Luke. (Lardner, part i. vol. ii. p. 768.) "Now in the fifteenth year of the reign of Tiberius Caesar,—Jesus began to be about thirty years of age:" for, supposing Jesus to have been born as Saint Matthew and Saint Luke relate, in the time of Herod, he must, according to the dates given in Josephus and by the Roman historians, have been at least thirty-one years of age in the fifteenth year of Tiberius. If he was born, as Saint Matthew's narrative intimates, one or two years before

---

* Josephus (Antiq. xvii. c. 2, sect. 6.) has this remarkable message: "When therefore the whole Jewish nation took an oath to be faithful to Caesar, and the interests of the king." This transaction corresponds in the course of the history with the time of Christ's birth. What is called a census was delivering upon oath an account of their property. This might be accompanied with an oath of fidelity, or might be mistaken by Josephus for it.

Herod's death, he would have been thirty-two or thirty-three years old at that time.

The solution turns upon an alteration in the construction of the Greek. Saint Luke's words in the original are allowed, by the general opinion of learned men, to signify, not "that Jesus began to be about thirty years of age," but "that he was about thirty years of age when he began his ministry." This construction being admitted, the adverb "about" gives us all the latitude we want.

III. Acts v. 36. "For before these days rose up Theudas, boasting himself to be somebody; to whom a number of men, about four hundred, joined themselves: who were slain; and all, as many as obeyed him, were scattered and brought to nought."

Josephus has preserved the account of an impostor of the name of Theudas, who was slain; but according to the date assigned to this man's appearance, (Michaelis's Introduction to the New Testament [Marsh's translation], vol. i. p. 61.) it must have been, at the least, seven years after Gamaliel's speech, of which this text is a part, was delivered. It has been replied to the objection, (Lardner, part i. vol. ii. p. 92.) that there might be two impostors of this name: and it has been observed that the same thing appears to have happened in other instances of the same kind. It is proved from Josephus, that there were not fewer than four persons of the name of Simon within forty years, and not fewer than three of the name of Judas within ten years, who were all leaders of insurrections: and that upon the death of Herod the Great there were innumerable disturbances in Judea. (Antiq. 1. 17, c. 12. sect. 4.)

IV. Matt. xxiii. 34. "Wherefore, behold I send unto you prophets, and wise men, and scribes, and some of them ye shall kill and crucify; and some of them shall ye scourge in your synagogues, and persecute them from city to city; that upon you may come all the righteous blood shed upon the earth, from the blood of righteous Abel unto the blood of Zacharias, son of Barachias, whom ye slew between the temple and the altar."

There is a Zacharias whose death is related in the second book of Chronicles,* in a manner which perfectly supports our Saviour's allusion. But this Zacharias was the son of Jehoiada.

There is also Zacharias the prophet; who was the son of Barachiah, and is so described in the superscription of his prophecy, but of whose death we have no account.

I have little doubt but that the first Zacharias was the person spoken of by our Saviour; and that the name of the father has been since added or changed, by some one who

---

* "And the Spirit of God came upon Zacharias, the son of Jehoiada the priest, which stood above the people, and bid unto them, Thus saith God, Why transgress ye the commandments of the Lord that ye cannot prosper? Because ye have forsaken the Lord, he hath also forsaken you. And they conspired against him, and stoned him with stones, at the commandment of the king, in the court of the house of the Lord." 2 Chron. xxiv. 20, 21.

took it from the title of the prophecy, which happened to be better known to him than the history in the Chronicles.

There is likewise a Zacharias, the son of Baruch, related by Josephus to have been slain in the temple a few years before the destruction of Jerusalem. It has been insinuated that the words put into our Saviour's mouth contain a reference to this transaction, and were composed by some writer who either confounded the time of the transaction with our Saviour's age, or inadvertently overlooked the anachronism.

Now, suppose it to have been so; suppose these words to have been suggested by the transaction related in Josephus, and to have been falsely ascribed to Christ; and observe what extraordinary coincidences attend the forger's mistake.

First, that we have a Zacharias in the book of Chronicles, whose death, and the manner of it, corresponds with the allusion.

Secondly, that although the name of this person's father be erroneously put down in the Gospel, yet we have a way of accounting for the error by showing another Zacharias in the Jewish Scriptures much better known than the former, whose patronymic was actually that which appears in the text.

Every one who thinks upon the subject will find these to be circumstances which could not have met together in a mistake which did not proceed from the circumstances themselves.

I have noticed, I think, all the difficulties of this kind. They are few: some of them admit of a clear, others of a probable solution.

## CHAPTER VII

# UNDESIGNED
# COINCIDENCES

Between the letters which bear the name of Saint Paul in our collection and his history in the Acts of the Apostles there exist many notes of correspondency. Neither the history was taken from the letters, nor the letters from the history. And the undesignedness of the agreements demonstrates that they have not been produced by any fraudulent contrivance. But coincidences, from which these causes are excluded, and which are too close and numerous to be accounted for by accidental concurrences of fiction, must necessarily have truth for their foundation. This argument appeared to my mind of so much value that I have pursued it through Saint Paul's thirteen epistles, in a work published by me, under the title of Horae Paulinae. I, therefore, refer the reader to Horae Pauline itself. And I would particularly invite his attention to the observations which are made upon the first three epistles.

It remains only, in this place, to point out how the argument bears upon the general question of the Christian history.

First, Saint Paul in these letters affirms his own performance of miracles, and, "That miracles were the signs of an Apostle." (Rom. xv. 18, 19. 2 Cor. xii. 12.) If this testimony come from Saint Paul's own hand, it is invaluable.

Secondly, it shows that the series of action represented in the epistles of Saint Paul was real; which alone lays a foundation for the proposition that the original witnesses of the Christian history devoted themselves to lives of toil, suffering, and danger, in consequence of their belief of the truth of that history, and for the sake of communicating the knowledge of it to others.

Thirdly, it proves that the author of the Acts of the Apostles, was well acquainted with Saint Paul's history; and that he probably was, what he professes himself to be, a companion of Saint Paul's travels; which, if true, establishes, in a considerable degree, the credit even of his Gospel, because it shows that the writer possessed opportunities of informing himself truly concerning the transactions which he relates. I have little difficulty in applying to the Gospel of Saint Luke what is proved concerning the Acts of the Apostles, considering them as two parts of the same history; for though there are instances of second parts being forgeries, I know none where the second part is genuine, and the first not so.

I will only observe, as a sequel of the argument, though not noticed in my work, the remarkable similitude between the style of Saint John's Gospel and of Saint John's Epistle. The style of Saint John's is not at all the style of Saint Paul's Epistles, nor is it the style of Saint James's or of Saint Peter's Epistles: but it bears a resemblance to the style of the Gospel inscribed with Saint John's name, so far as that resemblance can be expected to appear. Writings so circumstanced prove themselves, and one another, to be genuine. This correspondency is the more valuable, as the epistle itself asserts, in Saint John's manner, indeed, the writer's personal knowledge of Christ's history: "That which was from the beginning, which we have heard, which we have seen with our eyes, which we have looked upon, and our hands have handled, of the word of life; that which we have seen and heard, declare we unto you." (Ch. i. ver. 1–3.) Who perceives not the value of an account delivered by a writer so well informed as this?

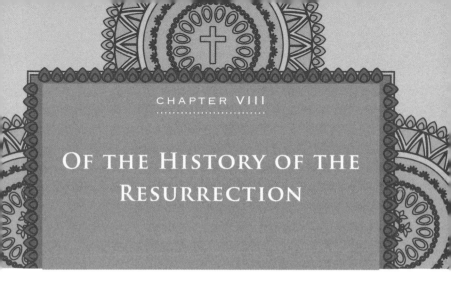

## CHAPTER VIII

# OF THE HISTORY OF THE RESURRECTION

The history of the resurrection of Christ is a part of the evidence of Christianity: but I do not know whether the proper strength, or wherein its peculiar value be generally understood. It is that it is completely certain that the apostles of Christ, and the first teachers of Christianity, asserted the fact. Every piece of Scripture recognizes the resurrection. Every epistle of every apostle, every author contemporary with the apostles, of the age immediately succeeding the apostles, every writing from that age to the present genuine or spurious, on the side of Christianity or against it, concur in representing the resurrection of Christ as an article of his history, received without doubt or disagreement by all who called themselves Christians, and alleged as the centre of their testimony. Nothing can be more certain than that his apostles, and the first teachers of Christianity, gave out that he did so. The only points which can enter into our consideration are, whether the apostles knowingly published a falsehood, or whether they were themselves deceived; whether either of these suppositions be possible. The first is pretty generally given up. The solution more deserving of notice is that which would resolve the conduct of the apostles into enthusiasm. There are circumstances in the narrative which destroy this comparison entirely. It was not one person but many, who saw him; they saw him not only separately but together, not only by night but by day, not at a distance but near, not once but several times; they not only saw him, but touched him, conversed with him, ate with him, examined his person to satisfy their doubts. These particulars are decisive: but they stand, I do admit, upon the credit of our records. I would answer, therefore, the insinuation of enthusiasm, by a circumstance which arises out of the nature of the thing; and the reality of which must be confessed by all who allow that the resurrection of Christ was asserted by his disciples from the beginning; and that circumstance is, the non-production of the dead body. It is related in the history that the corpse was missing out of the sepulchre: it is related also in the history, that the Jews reported that the followers of Christ had stolen it away.* And this account, though loaded with

---

* "And this saying," Saint Matthew writes, "is commonly reported amongst the Jews until this day" (chap. xxviii. 15). The evangelist may be thought good authority as to this point: and this point is sufficient to prove that the body was missing. It has been rightly, I

great improbabilities, such as the situation of the disciples, their fears for their own safety at the time, the unlikelihood of their expecting to succeed, the difficulty of actual success,[+] and the inevitable consequence of detection and failure, was, nevertheless, the most credible account that could be given of the matter. But it proceeds entirely upon the supposition of fraud, as all the old objections did. What account can be given of the body, upon the supposition of enthusiasm? It is impossible our Lord's followers could believe that he was risen from the dead, if his corpse was lying before them. All accounts of spectres leave the body in the grave. And although the body of Christ might be removed by fraud, and for the purposes of fraud, yet without any such intention, and by sincere but deluded men (which is the representation of the apostolic character we are now examining), no such attempt could be made. The presence and the absence of the dead body are alike inconsistent with the hypothesis of enthusiasm: for if present, it

---

think, observed by Dr. Townshend (Dis. upon the Res. p. 126), that the story of the guards carried collusion upon the face of it:—"His disciples came by night, and stole him away while we slept." Men in their circumstances would not have made such an acknowledgment of their negligence without previous assurances of protection and impunity.

[+] "Especially at the full moon, the city full of people, many probably passing the whole night, as Jesus and his disciples had done, in the open air, the sepulchre so near the city as to be now enclosed within the walls." Priestley on the Resurr. p. 24.

must have cured their enthusiasm at once; if absent, fraud, not enthusiasm, must have carried it away.

But further, if we admit so much of the account as states that the religion of Jesus was set up at Jerusalem, in the very place in which he had been buried, and a few days after he had been buried, his resurrection out of the grave, it is evident that, if his body could have been found, the Jews would have produced it, as the completest answer possible to the whole story. The attempt of the apostles could not have survived this refutation a moment. If we also admit, upon the authority of Saint Matthew, that the Jews were advertised of the expectation of Christ's followers, and that they had taken due precaution in consequence, and that the body was in marked and public custody, the observation receives more force still. For notwithstanding their precaution and although thus prepared and forewarned; when the story of the resurrection of Christ immediately came forth; when it was publicly asserted by his disciples, and made the ground and basis of their preaching in his name, and collecting followers to his religion, the Jews had not the body to produce; but were obliged to meet the testimony of the apostles by an answer inconsistent with the supposition which would resolve their conduct into enthusiasm.

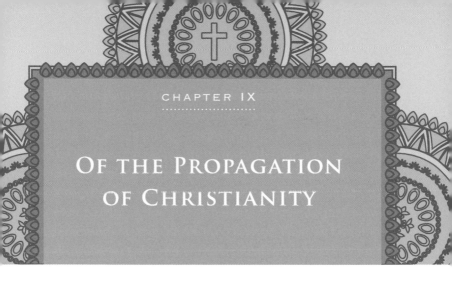

## CHAPTER IX

# OF THE PROPAGATION
# OF CHRISTIANITY

I n this argument, the first consideration is in what degree, within what time, and to what extent, Christianity actually was propagated.

The accounts of the matter which can be collected from our books are as follow: A few days after Christ's disappearance out of the world, we find an assembly of disciples at Jerusalem, to the number of "about one hundred and twenty;" (Acts i. 15.) which met together not merely as believers in Christ, but as personally connected with the apostles, and with one another. There is no proof that the followers of Christ were yet formed into a society; that the society was reduced into any order; that it was at this time even understood that a new religion was to be set up in the world. The death of Christ had left the generality of his disciples in great doubt, both as to what they were to do, and concerning what was to follow.

This meeting was holden a few days after Christ's ascension: for ten days after that event was the day of Pentecost, when, as our history relates, (Acts ii. 1.) upon a signal display of divine agency attending the persons of the apostles, there were added to the society "about three thousand souls." (Acts ii. 41.) But it is not, I think, that these three thousand were all converted by this single miracle; but rather that many who before were believers in Christ became now professors of Christianity.

We read in the fourth chapter (verse 4) of the Acts, that soon after this, "the number of the men," i. e. the society openly professing their belief in Christ, "was about five thousand." So that here is an increase of two thousand within a very short time. And it is probable that there were many who, although they believed in Christ, did not think it necessary to join themselves to this society; or who waited to see what was to become of it. Gamaliel, whose advice to the Jewish council is recorded Acts v. 34, appears to have been of this description; perhaps Nicodemus, and perhaps also Joseph of Arimathea. This class of men are likewise pointed out by Saint John, in the twelfth chapter of his Gospel: "Nevertheless, among the chief rulers also many believed on him, but because of the Pharisees they did not confess him, lest they should be put out of the synagogue, for they loved the praise of men more than the praise of God." Persons such as these might admit the miracles of Christ, without being immediately convinced that they were under obligation to make a public profession of Christianity at the risk of all that was dear to them in life, and even of life itself.*

Christianity proceeded to increase in Jerusalem by a progress equally rapid with its first success; for in the next chapter of our history, we read that "believers were the more added to the Lord, multitudes both of men and women." And this enlargement appears in the first verse of the succeeding chapter, wherein we are told, that "when the number of the disciples was multiplied, there arose a murmuring of the Grecians against the Hebrews because their widows were neglected;" (Acts v. 14; vi. 1) and afterwards, it is declared expressly, that "the number of the disciples

---

* "Beside those who professed, and those who rejected and opposed, Christianity, there were in all probability multitudes between both, neither perfect Christians nor yet unbelievers. They had a favourable opinion of the Gospel, but worldly considerations made them unwilling to own it. There were many circumstances which inclined them to think that Christianity was a divine revelation, but there were many inconveniences which attended the open profession of it; and they could not find in themselves courage enough to bear them to disoblige their friends and family, to ruin their fortunes, to lose their reputation, their liberty, and their life, for the sake of the new religion. Therefore they were willing to hope, that if they endeavoured to observe the great principles of morality which Christ had represented as the principal part, the sum and substance of religion; if they thought honourably of the Gospel; if they offered no injury to the Christians; if they did them all the services that they could safely perform, they were willing to hope that God would accept this, and that He would excuse and forgive the rest." Jortin's Dis. on the Christ. Rel. p. 91, ed. 4.

multiplied in Jerusalem greatly, and that a great company of the priests were obedient to the faith."

This I call the first period in the propagation of Christianity. It commences with the ascension of Christ, and extends to something more than one year after that event. During which term, the preaching of Christianity was confined to the single city of Jerusalem.

By reason of a persecution, the converts were driven from that city, and dispersed throughout the regions of Judea and Samaria. (Acts viii. 1.) Wherever they came, they brought their religion with them: for our historian informs us, (Acts viii. 4.) that "they that were scattered abroad went everywhere preaching the word." The effect of this preaching comes afterwards to be noticed, where the historian is led to observe that then (i. e. about three years posterior to this, [Benson, b. i. p. 207.]) the churches had rest throughout all Judea and Galilee and Samaria. This was the work of the second period, which comprises about four years.

Hitherto the preaching of the Gospel had been confined to Jews, to Jewish proselytes, and to Samaritans. It was not yet known to the apostles that they were at liberty to propose the religion to mankind at large. That "mystery," as Saint Paul calls it, (Eph. iii. 3–6.) was revealed to Peter by an especial miracle. It appears to have been (Benson, book ii. p. 236.) about seven years after Christ's ascension that the Gospel was preached to the Gentiles of Cesarea. A year after this a great multitude of Gentiles were converted at Antioch in Syria:—"A great number believed, and turned to the Lord;" "much people was added unto the Lord;" "the apostles Barnabas and Paul taught much people." (Acts xi. 21, 24, 26.) Upon Herod's death, which happened in the next year, (Benson, book ii, p. 289.) "the word of God grew and multiplied." (Acts xii. 24.) Three years from this time, upon the preaching of Paul at Iconium, the metropolis of Lycaonia, "a great multitude both of Jews and Greeks believed:" (Acts xiv. 1.) and afterwards, in the course of this very progress, he is represented as "making many disciples" at Derbe, a principal city in the same district. Three years (Benson's History of Christ, book iii. p. 50.) after this, which brings us to sixteen after the ascension, the apostles wrote a public letter from Jerusalem to the Gentile converts in Antioch, Syria, and Cilicia, with which letter Paul travelled through these countries, and found the churches "established in the faith, and increasing in number daily." (Acts xvi. 5.) From Asia the apostle proceeded into Greece, where we find him at Thessalonica: in which city, "some of the Jews believed, and of the devout Greeks a great multitude." (Acts xvii. 4.) At Berea, the next city at which Saint Paul arrives, the historian, who was present, inform us that "many of the Jews believed." (Acts xvii. 12.) The next year and a half of Saint Paul's ministry was spent at Corinth. Of his success in that city we receive the following intimations; "that many of the Corinthians believed and were baptized;" and "that it was revealed to the Apostle by Christ, that he had much people in that city." (Acts xviii, 8–10.) Within less than twenty-five (Benson, book iii. p, 160.) years after the ascension, Saint Paul fixed his station at Ephesus for the space of two years. (Acts xix. 10.) The effect of his ministry in that city and neighbourhood drew from the historian a reflection how "mightily grew the word of God and prevailed." (Acts xix. 20.) And at the conclusion of this period we find Demetrius at the head of a party, who were alarmed by the progress of the religion, complaining, that "not only at Ephesus, but also throughout all Asia (i. e. the province of Lydia, and the country adjoining to Ephesus), this Paul hath persuaded and turned away much people." (Acts xix. 26.) Beside these, there occurs mention of converts at Rome, Alexandria, Athens, Cyprus, Cyrene, Macedonia, Philippi.

This is the third period in the propagation of Christianity, setting off in the seventh year after the ascension, and ending at the twenty-eighth. During all this time Jerusalem continued not only the centre of the mission, but a principal seat of the religion; for when Saint Paul returned thither at the conclusion of the period of which we are now considering, the other apostles pointed out to him, "how many thousands (myriads, ten thousands) there were in that city who believed."*

Upon this abstract, and the writing from which it is drawn, the following observations seem material to be made:

I. That the account comes from a person who
was concerned in a portion of what he relates,

---

* Acts xxi. 20.

and was contemporary with the whole of it; who visited Jerusalem, and frequented the society of those who were acting the chief parts in the transaction.

II. That this account is a very incomplete account of the propagation of Christianity; that if what we read in the history be true, much more than what the history contains must be true also. For the narrative is, in fact, a history of the twelve apostles only during a short time of their continuing together at Jerusalem; and even of this period the account is very concise. The work afterwards consists of a few important passages of Peter's ministry, of the speech and death of Stephen, of the preaching of Philip the deacon; and the conversion, the travels, the discourses, and history of the new apostle, Paul; in which history, also, large portions of time are often passed over.

III. That the account is for this very reason more credible. Had it been the author's design to have displayed the early progress of Christianity, he would undoubtedly have set forth accounts of the preaching of the rest of the apostles, who cannot be supposed to have remained silent and inactive, or not to

have met with a share of that success which
attended their colleagues.

To which may be added

IV. That the intimations of the number of
converts, and of the success of the preaching
of the apostles, come out for the most part
incidentally: are drawn from the historian
by the occasion. All this tends to remove the
suspicion of a design to exaggerate or deceive.

*Parallel testimonies* with the history are the letters of Saint
Paul, and of the other apostles. Those of Saint Paul are
addressed to the churches of Corinth, Philippi, Thessalonica,
the church of Galatia, and, of Ephesus; his ministry at all
which places is recorded in the history: to the churches of
Colosse and Laodicea jointly, which he had not then visited. They recognise by reference the churches of Judea, the
churches of Asia, and "all the churches of the Gentiles."
(Thess ii. 14.) In the Epistle to the Romans (Rom. xv. 18,
19.) the author delivers a remarkable declaration,—"to make
the Gentiles obedient by word and deed, through mighty
signs and wonders, by the power of the Spirit of God; so
that from Jerusalem, and round about unto Illyricum, I have
fully preached the Gospel of Christ." In the epistle to the
Colossians, (Col. i. 23.) we find a very strong signification
of the then state of the Christian mission as it appeared to

Saint Paul:—"If ye continue in the faith, grounded and settled, and be not moved away from the hope of the Gospel,
which ye have heard, and which was preached to every
creature which is under heaven;" which Gospel, he had
reminded them near the beginning of his letter (Col. i. 6.),
"was present with them, as it was in all the world." The first
epistle of Peter accosts the Christians dispersed throughout
Pontus, Galatia, Cappadocia, Asia, and Bithynia.

It comes next to be considered how far these accounts
are confirmed by other evidence.

Tacitus, in delivering a relation of the fire which happened at Rome in the tenth year of Nero, asserts that the
emperor, in order to suppress the rumours of having been
himself the author of the mischief, procured the Christians
to be accused. Of which Christians the following is the historian's account as belongs to our present purpose: "They
had their denomination from Christus, who, in the reign
of Tiberius, was put to death as a criminal by the procurator Pontius Pilate. This pernicious superstition, though
checked for a while, broke out again, and spread not only
over Judea, but reached the city also. At first they only were
apprehended who confessed themselves of that sect; afterwards vast multitude were discovered by them." This testimony is from an historian of great reputation, living near the
time; from an enemy to the religion; and it joins immediately with the period through which the Scripture accounts
extend. It establishes that the religion began at Jerusalem;
that it spread throughout Judea; that it had reached Rome,

and that it had there obtained a great number of converts. This was about six years after the time that Saint Paul wrote his Epistle to the Romans. The converts to the religion were then so numerous at Rome, that of those who were betrayed by the information of the persons first persecuted, a great multitude (multitudo ingens) were discovered and seized.

It seems probable, that the temporary check which Tacitus represents Christianity to have received (repressa in praesens) referred to the persecution of Jerusalem which followed the death of Stephen (Acts viii.); and which, by dispersing the converts, caused the institution, in some measure, to disappear. Its second eruption at the same place, and within a short time, has much in it of the character of truth.

Next in order of time, is the testimony of Pliny the Younger. Pliny was the Roman governor of Pontus and Bithynia, two considerable districts in the northern part of Asia Minor. The situation in his province led him to apply to the emperor (Trajan) for his direction as to the conduct he was to hold towards the Christians. The letter was written not quite eighty years after Christ's ascension. The president, in this letter, states the measures he had already pursued, and then adds:—"Suspending all judicial proceedings, I have recourse to you for advice; for it has appeared to me a matter highly deserving consideration, especially on account of the great number of persons who are in danger of suffering: for many of all ages, and of every rank, of both sexes likewise, are accused, and will be accused. Nor has the contagion of this superstition seized cities only, but the lesser towns also, and the open country. Nevertheless it seemed to me that it may be restrained and corrected. It is certain that the temples, which were almost forsaken, begin to be more frequented; and the sacred solemnities, after a long intermission, are revived. Victims, likewise, are everywhere (passim) bought up; whereas, for some time, there were few to purchase them. Whence it is easy to imagine that numbers of men might be reclaimed if pardon were granted to those that shall repent." (C. Plin. Trajano Imp. lib. x. ep. xcvii.)

The passage of Pliny's letter here quoted, proves, not only that the Christians in Pontus and Bithynia were now numerous, but that they had subsisted there for some considerable time. There are also two clauses in the former part of the letter which indicate the same thing; one, in which he declares that he had "never been present at any trials of Christians, and therefore knew not what was the usual subject of inquiry and punishment, or how far either was wont to be urged." The second clause is the following: "Others were named by an informer, who, at first, confessed themselves Christians, and afterwards denied it; the rest said they had been Christians some three years ago, some longer, and some about twenty years." Pliny speaks of the Christians as a description of men well known to the person to whom he writes.

Here then is a very singular evidence of the progress of the Christian religion in a short space. It was not fourscore years after the crucifixion of Jesus when Pliny wrote this letter. Bithynia and Pontus were at a great distance from Judea;

yet in these provinces Christianity had long subsisted.

Certainly, this letter may fairly be applied in confirmation of the representations given of the general state of Christianity in the world, by Christian writers of that and the next succeeding age.

Justin Martyr, who wrote about thirty years after Pliny, and one hundred and six after the ascension, has these remarkable words: "There is not a nation, either of Greek or barbarian, or of any other name, even of those who wander in tribes, and live in tents, amongst whom prayers and thanksgivings are not offered to the Father and Creator of the universe by the name of the crucified Jesus." (Dial cum Tryph.) Tertullian, who comes about fifty years after Justin, appeals to the governors of the Roman empire: "We were but of yesterday, and we have filled your cities, islands, towns, and boroughs, the camp, the senate, and the forum. They (the heathen adversaries of Christianity) lament that every sex, age, and condition, and persons of every rank also, are converts to that name." (Tertull. Apol. c. 37.) This public boasting upon a subject which must be known to every reader was not only useless but unnatural, unless the truth of the case corresponded with the description. The same Tertullian, in another passage, enumerates as belonging to Christ, beside many other countries, the "Moors and Gaetulians of Africa, the borders of Spain, several nations of France, and parts of Britain inaccessible to the Romans, the Sarmatians, Daci, Germans, and Scythians;" (Ad Jud. c. 7.) and the number of Christians in the several countries in which it prevailed is thus expressed by him: "Although so great a multitude, that in almost every city we form the greater part, we pass our time modestly and in silence." (Ad Scap. c. iii.) A Clemens Alexandrinus, who preceded Tertullian by a few years, introduced a comparison between the success of Christianity and that of the most celebrated philosophical institutions: "The philosophers were confined to Greece, and to their particular retainers; but the doctrine of the Master of Christianity not remain in Judea, as philosophy did in Greece, but is throughout the whole world, in every nation, and village, and city, both of Greeks and barbarians, converting both whole houses and separate individuals, having already brought over to the truth not a few of the philosophers themselves. If the Greek philosophy he prohibited, it immediately vanishes; whereas, from the first preaching of our doctrine, kings and tyrants, governors and presidents, with their whole train, and with the populace on their side, have endeavoured with their whole might to exterminate it, yet doth it flourish more and more." (Clem. Al. Strora. lib. vi. ad fin.) Origen, who follows Tertullian at the distance of only thirty years, delivers nearly the same account: "In every part of the world," says he, "throughout all Greece, and in all other nations, there are innumerable and immense multitudes, who, having left the laws of their country, and those whom they esteemed gods, have given themselves up to the law of Moses, and the religion of Christ: and this not without the bitterest resentment from the idolaters, by whom they were frequently put to torture, and sometimes to death: and it is wonderful to observe how, in so short a time, the religion has increased, amidst punishment and death, and every kind of torture." (Orig. in Cels. lib. i.)

Less than eighty years after this, the Roman empire became Christian under Constantine: and it is probable that Constantine declared himself on the side of the Christians because they were the powerful party: for Arnobius, who wrote immediately before Constantine's accession, speaks of "the whole world as filled with Christ's doctrine, of its diffusion throughout all countries, of an innumerable body of Christians in distant provinces, of the strange revolution of opinion of men of the greatest genius,—orators, grammarians, rhetoricians, lawyers, physicians having come over to the institution, and that also in the face of threats, executions and tortures." (Arnob. in Genres, 1. i. pp. 27, 9, 24, 42, 41. edit. Lug. Bat. 1650.)

And not more than twenty years after Constantine's entire possession of the empire, Julius Firmiens Maternus calls upon the emperors Constantius and Constans to extirpate the relics of the fallen ancient religion. Fifty years afterwards, Jerome represents the decline of Paganism: "Solitudinem patitur et in urbe gentilitas. Dii quondam nationum, cum bubonibus et noctuis, in solis culminibus remanserunt." (Jer. ad Lect. ep. 5, 7.) Jerome here indulges a triumph, which could only be suggested to his mind by the universality with which he saw; the religion received. Were, therefore, the motives of Constantine's conversion ever so problematical, the easy establishment of Christianity, and the ruin of Heathenism, under him and his immediate successors, is of itself a proof of the progress which had made in the preceding period.

## SECTION II

### REFLECTIONS UPON THE PRECEDING ACCOUNT

In viewing the progress of Christianity, our first attention is due to the number of converts at Jerusalem, immediately after its Founder's death; because this was a success at the time, and upon the spot, when and where the chief part of the history had been transacted.

We are, in the next place, called upon to attend to the early establishment of numerous Christian societies in Judea and Galilee; which countries had been the scene of Christ's miracles and ministry, and where the memory must have yet been fresh and certain.

We are, thirdly, invited to recollect the success of the apostles and of their companions, at the several places to which they came; because it was the credit given to original witnesses, appealing for the truth of what themselves had seen and heard. The effect of their preaching strongly confirms that they were able to exhibit to their hearers supernatural attestations of their mission.

We are, lastly, to consider the subsequent growth and spread of the religion, of which we receive successive intimations, and satisfactory accounts, until its full and final establishment.

In all these several stages, the history is without a parallel. "To establish a new religion, even amongst a few people, or in one single nation, is a thing in itself exceedingly difficult. To reform some corruptions which may have spread in a religion, or to make new regulations in it, is not perhaps so hard, when the main and principal part of that religion is preserved entire and unshaken; and yet this very often cannot be accomplished without an extraordinary concurrence of circumstances, and may be attempted a thousand times without success. But to introduce a new faith, a new way of thinking and acting, and to persuade many nations to quit the religion in which their ancestors have lived and died, which had been delivered down to them from time immemorial; to make them forsake and despise the deities which they had been accustomed to reverence and worship; this is a work of still greater difficulty." (Jortin's Dis. on the Christ. Rel. p. 107, 4th edit.) The resistance of education, worldly policy, and superstition, is almost invincible.

If men, in these days, be Christians in consequence of their education, in submission to authority, or in compliance with fashion, let us recollect that the very contrary of this, at the beginning, was the case. The first race of Christians, as well as millions who succeeded them, became such in formal opposition to all these motives. Every argument, therefore, and every instance, which sets forth the prejudice of education, and the almost irresistible effects of that prejudice, in fact confirms the evidence of Christianity.

But, in order to judge of the argument which is drawn from the early propagation of Christianity, I know no fairer way than to compare what we have seen with the success of Christian missions in modern ages.* In the East India mission, we hear sometimes of thirty or forty being baptized in the course of a year, and these principally children. Of adults voluntarily embracing Christianity, the number is extremely small. "Notwithstanding the labour of missionaries for upwards of two hundred years, and the establishments of different Christian nations who support them, there are not twelve thousand Indian Christians, and those almost entirely outcasts." (Sketches relating to the history, learning, and manners of the Hindoos, p. 48; quoted by Dr. Robertson, Hist. Dis. concerning Ancient India, p. 236.)

I lament the little progress which Christianity has made in these countries; but I see in it a strong proof of the Divine origin of the religion. What had the apostles to assist them in propagating Christianity which the missionaries have not? If piety and zeal had been sufficient, our missionaries possess these qualities in a high degree. If the intrinsic excellency of the religion, the perfection of its morality, the purity of its precepts, were the recommendations by which it made its way, these remain the same. If the character and circumstances under which the preachers were introduced to the countries be accounted of importance, this advantage

---

* [This is referring to the 1850s.]

is all on the side of the modern missionaries. They come from a country and a people to which the Indian world look up with sentiments of deference. The apostles came forth amongst the Gentiles under no other name than that of Jews, which was precisely the character they despised and derided. If it be disgraceful in India to become a Christian, it could not be much less so to be enrolled amongst those "quos, per flagitia invisos, vulgus Christianos appellabat." If the religion which they had to encounter be considered, the difference will not be great. The theology of both was nearly the same. The sacred rites of the Western Polytheism were gay, festive, and licentious; the rites of the public religion in the East partake of the same character.

On both sides of the comparison, the popular religion had a strong establishment. In ancient Greece and Rome it was strictly incorporated with the state. In India, a powerful and numerous caste possesses exclusively the administration of the established worship; and are, of consequence, devoted to its service, and attached to its interest. In both, the origin of the tradition is run up into ages long anterior to the existence of credible history, or of written language. In both, the established superstition was credited by the bulk of the people, but by the learned and philosophical part of the community either derided, or regarded by them as only fit to be upholden for the sake of its political uses.*

---

* "How absurd soever the articles of faith may be which superstition has adopted, or how unhallowed the rites which it prescribes, the former are received, in every age and country with unhesitating assent, by

We have particularly directed our observations to the progress of Christianity amongst the inhabitants of India: but the history of the Christian mission in other countries presents the same idea as the Indian mission does of the feebleness and inadequacy of human means.

From the widely disproportionate effects which attend the preaching of modern missionaries of Christianity, compared with what followed the ministry of Christ and his apostles under circumstances not so unlike as to account for the difference, a conclusion is fairly drawn in support of what our histories deliver concerning them, viz. that they had proofs to appeal to which we want.

---

the great body of the people, and the latter observed with scrupulous exactness. In our reasonings concerning opinions and practices which differ widely from our own, we are extremely apt to err. Having been instructed ourselves in the principles of a religion worthy in every respect of that Divine wisdom by which they were dictated, we frequently express wonder at the credulity of nations, in embracing systems of belief which appear to us so directly repugnant to right reason; and sometimes suspect that tenets so wild and extravagant do not really gain credit with them. But experience may satisfy us, that neither our wonder nor suspicions are well founded. No article of the public religion was called in question by those people of ancient Europe with whose history we are best acquainted; and no practice which it enjoined appeared improper to them. On the other hand, every opinion that tended to diminish the reverence of men for the gods of their country, or to alienate them from their worship, excited, among the Greeks and Romans, that indignant zeal which is natural to every people attached to their religion by a firm persuasion of its truth." Ind. Dis. p. 321.

## SECTION III

## OF THE RELIGION OF MAHOMET

The only event in the history of the human species which admits of comparison with the propagation of Christianity is the success of Mahometanism. The Mahometan institution was rapid in its progress, was recent in its history, and was founded upon a supernatural or prophetic character assumed by its author. In these articles, the resemblance with Christianity is confessed. But there are points of difference which separate the two cases entirely.

I. Mahomet did not found his pretensions upon proofs of supernatural agency capable of being known and attested by others. By the evidence of the Koran, Mahomet not only does not affect the power of working miracles, but expressly disclaims it.

The only place in the Koran in which it can be pretended that a sensible miracle is referred to is the beginning of the fifty-fourth chapter. The words are these:—"The hour of judgment approacheth, and the moon hath been split in sunder: but if the unbelievers see a sign, they turn aside, saying, This is a powerful charm." The Mahometan expositors disagree in their interpretation of this passage; some explaining it to be mention of the splitting of the moon as one of the future signs of the approach of the day of judgment: others referring it to a miraculous appearance which had then taken place. (Vide Sale, in loc.) It seems not improbable, that Mahomet might have taken advantage of some unusual appearance of the moon, which had happened about this time; and which supplied a foundation both for this passage, and for the story which in after times had been raised out of it.

From comparing what Mahomet himself wrote and said with what was afterwards reported of him by his followers, the plain and fair conclusion is, that when the religion was established by conquest, then, and not till then, came out the stories of his miracles.

Now this difference alone constitutes a bar to all reasoning from one case to the other. The success of a religion founded upon a miraculous history shows the credit which was given to the history; and this credit, under the circumstances in which it was given, is evidence of the reality of the history, and, by consequence, of the truth of the religion. We admit that multitudes acknowledged the pretensions of Mahomet: but, these pretensions being destitute of miraculous evidence, could not be secure grounds of persuasion to his followers, nor their example any authority to us. Admit the whole of Mahomet's authentic history, so far as it was of a nature capable of being known or witnessed by others, to be true and Mahomet might still be an impostor, or enthusiast, or a union of both. Admit to be true almost any part of Christ's history which was public, and he must have come from God.

II. The establishment of Mahomet's religion was affected by causes which in no degree appertained to the origin of Christianity.

During the first twelve years of his mission, Mahomet had recourse only to persuasion. "Three years were silently employed in the conversion of fourteen proselytes. For ten years, the religion advanced with a slow and painful progress, within the walls of Mecca. The number of proselytes in the seventh year of his mission may be estimated by the absence of eighty-three men and eighteen women, who retired to Aethiopia." (Gibbon's Hist. vol. ix. p. 244, et seq. ed. Dub.) Yet this progress, such as it was, appears to have been aided by some very important advantages which Mahomet found in his situation, in his mode of conducting his design, and in his doctrine.

1.  Mahomet was the grandson of the most powerful and honourable family in Mecca; and had an opulent marriage. A person considerable by his wealth, of high descent, and nearly allied to the chiefs of his country, taking upon himself the character of a religious teacher, would not fail of attracting attention and followers.

2. Mahomet conducted his design with great art and prudence. His first application was to his own family. He next expressed himself to Abu Beer, a man amongst the first of the Koreish

in wealth and influence. Abu Beer drew in five other principal persons in Mecca, whose solicitations prevailed upon five more of the same rank. Upon the strength of these allies, and under the powerful protection of his family, Mahomet now commenced his public preaching. And the advance which he made during the nine or ten remaining years of his peaceable ministry was by no means greater than what might reasonably have been expected. How soon his primitive adherents were let into the secret of his views of empire it is not now easy to determine. The event however was, that these, his first proselytes, all ultimately attained to riches and honours, to the command of armies, and the government of kingdoms. (Gibbon, vol. ix. p 244.)

3. The Arabs deduced their descent from Abraham through the line of Ishmael. The inhabitants of Mecca, in common probably with the other Arabian tribes, acknowledged one supreme Deity, but had associated with him many objects of idolatrous worship. The great doctrine with which Mahomet set out was the strict and exclusive unity of God. Abraham, he told them, their illustrous ancestor; Ishmael, the father of their nation; Moses, the lawgiver of the Jews; and Jesus, the author of Christianity—had all

asserted the same thing; that their followers had universally corrupted the truth, and that he was now commissioned to restore it to the world.

4.  Of the institution which Mahomet joined with this fundamental doctrine, and of the Koran in which that institution is delivered, two purposes pervade the whole, viz., to make converts, and to make his converts soldiers. The following particulars, amongst others, may be considered as pretty evident indications of these designs:

    1. When Mahomet began to preach, his address to the Jews, to the Christians, and to the Pagan Arabs, was, that the religion which he taught was no other than what had been originally their own. "He hath ordained you the religion which he commanded Noah, and which we have revealed unto thee, O Mohammed, and which we commanded Abraham, and Moses, and Jesus, saying, Observe this religion, and be not divided therein." (Sale's Koran, c. xlii. p. 393.)

    2. The author of the Koran never ceases from describing the future anguish of unbelievers, their despair, regret, penitence, and torment. The terror which they seem well calculated to inspire would be to many tempers a powerful application.

3. On the other hand: his voluptuous paradise; his robes of silk, his palaces of marble, his riven, and shades, his groves and couches, his wines, his dainties; and, above all, his seventy-two virgins assigned to each of the faithful, of resplendent beauty and eternal youth—intoxicated the imaginations of his Eastern followers.

4. But Mahomet's highest heaven was reserved for those who fought his battles or expended their fortunes in his cause: "Those believers who sit still at home, not having any hurt, and those who employ their fortunes and their persons for the religion of God, shall not be held equal. God hath preferred those who employ their fortunes and their persons in that cause to a degree above those who sit at home. God had indeed promised every one Paradise; but God had preferred those who fight for the faith before those who sit still, by adding unto them a great reward; by degrees of honour conferred upon them from him, and by granting them forgiveness and mercy." (Sale's Koran, c. iv. p. 73.)

5. His doctrine of predestination was applied by him to the same purpose of fortifying and of exalting the courage of his adherents.—"If anything of the matter had

happened unto us, we had not been slain here.
Answer; If ye had been in your houses, verily
they would have gone forth to fight, whose
slaughter was decreed, to the places where they
died." (Sale's Koran, c. iii. p. 54.)

6. In warm regions, the appetite of the
sexes is ardent, the passion for inebriating
liquors moderate. Although Mahomet laid a
restraint upon the drinking of wine, in the use
of women he allowed an almost unbounded
indulgence. Four wives, with the liberty of
changing them at pleasure, (Sale's Koran,
c. iv. p. 63.) together with the persons of all
his captives, (Gibbon, vol. ix. p. 225.) was an
irresistible bribe to an Arabian warrior. "God is
minded," says he, speaking of this very subject,
"to make his religion light unto you; for man
was created weak."

What has hitherto been collected from the records of
the Musselman history relates to the twelve or thirteen
years of Mahomet's peaceable preaching, which part alone
of his life and enterprise admits of the smallest comparison with the origin of Christianity. A new scene is now
unfolded. The city of Medina, distant about ten days' journey from Mecca, was at that time distracted by the heredi-
tary contentions of two hostile tribes. (Mod. Univ. Hist.
Vol. i. p. 100.) The religion of Mahomet presented, in some

measure, a point of union or compromise to these divided opinions. It embraced the principles which were common to them all. It was not a religious, but a political association, which ultimately introduced Mahomet into Medina. After an embassy, therefore, composed of believers and unbelievers, (Mod. Univ. Hist. Vol. i, p. 85.) and of persons of both tribes, with whom a treaty was concluded of strict alliance and support, Mahomet made his public entry, and was received as the sovereign of Medina.

Having now a town at his command, where to arm his party, he enters upon new counsels. He now pretends that a divine commission is given him to attack the infidels, to destroy idolatry, and to set up the true faith by the sword. (Mod. Univ. Hist. Vol. i. p. 88.) An early victory over a very superior force, achieved by conduct and bravery, established the renown of his arms, and of his personal character. (Victory of Bedr, Mod. Univ. Hist. Vol. i. p. 106.) Every year after this was marked by battles or assassinations.

From this time we have nothing left to account for, but that Mahomet should collect an army, that his army should conquer, and that his religion should proceed together with his conquests. From all sides, the roving Arabs crowded round the standard of religion and plunder, of freedom and victory, of arms and rapine. Beside the highly painted joys of a carnal paradise, Mahomet rewarded his followers in this world with a liberal division of the spoils, and with the persons of their female captives. (Gibbon, vol. ix. p. 255.) That Mahomet's conquests should carry his religion along with them will excite little surprise, when we know death or conversion was the only choice offered to idolaters. "Strike off their heads! strike off all the ends of their fingers! (Sale's Koran, c. viii. p. 140.) kill the idolaters, wheresoever ye shall find them!" (Sale's Koran, c. ix. p. 149.) To the Jews and Christians was left the somewhat milder alternative of subjection and tribute, if they persisted in their own religion. "Ye Christian dogs, you know your option; the Koran, the tribute, or the sword." (Gibbon, vol. ix. p. 337.) The corrupted state of Christianity in the seventh century, unhappily so fell in with men's care of their safety or their fortunes, as to induce many to forsake its profession. Add to all which, that Mahomet's victories were constantly represented as divine declarations in his favour. Success was evidence. Prosperity carried with it, not only influence, but proof.

Many more passages might be collected out of the Koran to the same effect; but they are unnecessary. The success of Mahometanism during this, and every future period of its history, bears so little resemblance to the early propagation of Christianity, that no inference whatever can justly be drawn from it to the prejudice of the Christian argument. The success, therefore, of Mahometanism stands not in the way of this important conclusion; that the propagation of Christianity, in the manner and under the circumstances in which it was propagated, is an unique in the history of the species. A Jewish peasant overthrew the religion of the world.

PART III

# A BRIEF CONSIDERATION OF SOME POPULAR OBJECTIONS

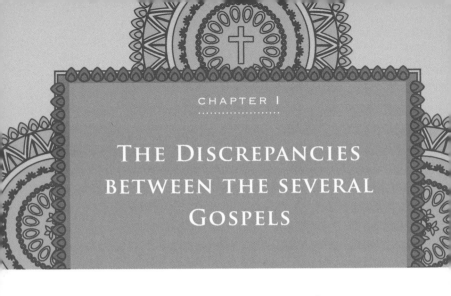

## CHAPTER 1

# THE DISCREPANCIES BETWEEN THE SEVERAL GOSPELS

The usual character of human testimony is substantial truth under circumstantial variety. When written histories touch upon the same scenes of action; numerous, and sometimes important, variations present themselves; not seldom, also, absolute and final contradictions; yet neither one nor the other are deemed sufficient to shake the credibility of the main fact. The embassy of the Jews to deprecate the execution of Claudian's order to place his statue, in their temple, Philo places in harvest, Josephus in seed time; both contemporary writers. No reader is led by this inconsistency to doubt whether such an embassy was sent, or whether such an order was given. Yet this ought to be left in uncertainty, according to the principles upon which the Christian history has sometimes been attacked. Dr. Middleton contended, that the different hours of the day assigned to the crucifixion of Christ, by John and by the other Evangelists, did not admit of the reconcilement which learned men had proposed: and then concludes the discussion with this hard remark; "We must be forced, with several of the critics, to leave the difficulty just as we found it, chargeable with all the consequences of manifest inconsistency." (Middleton's Reflections answered by Benson, Hist. Christ. vol. iii. p. 50.) But what are these consequences? By no means the discrediting of the history as to the principal fact, by a repugnancy in the time of the day in which it is said to have taken place.

A great deal of the discrepancy observable in the Gospels arises from omission; from a fact or a passage of Christ's life being noticed by one writer which is unnoticed by another. We perceive it, not only in the comparison of different writers, but even in the same writer when compared with himself. There are a great many particulars mentioned by Josephus in his Antiquities, which, as we should have supposed, ought to have been put down by him in their place in the Jewish Wars. (Lardner, part i. vol. ii. p. 735, et seq.) Suetonius, Tacitus, Dio Cassius, have, all three, written of the reign of Tiberius. Each has mentioned many things omitted by the rest, (Lardner, part i. vol. ii. p. 743.) yet no objection is from thence taken to the respective credit of their histories.

But these discrepancies will be still more numerous, when men write memoirs: which is, perhaps, the proper description of our Gospels: that is, when they never meant to deliver a complete account of all the things of importance which the person who is the subject of their history did or said; but only, out of many similar ones, to give such passages, or such actions and discourses, as offered themselves more immediately to their attention, came in the way of their inquiries, occurred to their recollection, or were suggested by their particular design at the time of writing.

This particular design may appear sometimes, but not always, nor often. Thus I think that the particular design which Saint Matthew had in view whilst he was writing the history of the resurrection was to attest the faithful performance of Christ's promise to his disciples to go before them into Galilee; because he has recorded this promise, and he alone has confined his narrative to that single appearance to the disciples which fulfilled it. It was the thing which dwelt upon Saint Matthew's mind, and he adapted his narrative to it. But, that there is nothing in Saint Matthew's language which negatives other appearances, or which imports that this his appearance to his disciples in Galilee, was his first or only appearance, is made pretty evident by Saint Mark's Gospel, which uses the same terms concerning the appearance in Galilee as Saint Matthew uses, yet itself records two other appearances prior to this: "Go your way, tell his disciples and Peter, that he goeth before you into Galilee: there shall ye see him as he said unto you" (xvi. 7). We might be apt to infer from these words, that this was the first time they were to see him; at least, we might infer it, with as much reason as we draw the inference from the same words in Matthew: the historian himself did not perceive that he was leading his readers to any such conclusion; for, in the twelfth and following verses of this chapter, he informs us of two appearances, which, by comparing the order of events, are shown to have been prior to the appearance in Galilee. "He appeared in another form unto two of them, as they walked, and went into the country; and they went and told it unto the residue, neither believed they them: afterwards he appeared unto the eleven, as they sat at meat, and upbraided them with their unbelief, because they believed not them that had seen him after he was risen."

Probably the same observation, concerning the particular design which guided the historian, may be of use in comparing many other passages of the Gospels.

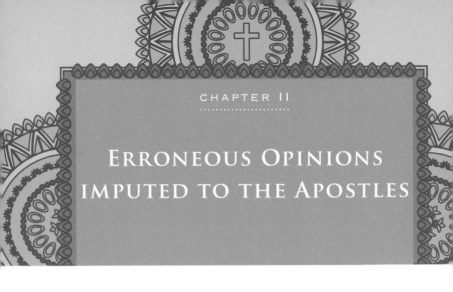

# ERRONEOUS OPINIONS
# IMPUTED TO THE APOSTLES

A species of candour which is shown towards every other book is sometimes refused to the Scriptures: the placing of a distinction between judgment and testimony. We do not usually question the credit of a writer, by reason of an opinion he may have delivered upon subjects unconnected with his evidence: we naturally separate facts from opinions.

To apply this equitable consideration to the Christian records, much controversy and much objection has been raised concerning the quotations of the Old Testament found in the New; some of which are applied in a sense and to events apparently different from those to which they belong in the original. It is probable that many of those quotations were intended by the writers of the New Testament as nothing more than accommodations. They quoted passages of their Scripture which suited the occasion before them, without always undertaking to assert that the occasion was in the view of the author of the words. Such accommodations of passages from books especially which are in every one's hands, are common with writers of all countries. Those prophecies which are alleged with more solemnity, and which are accompanied with a precise declaration that they originally respected the event then related, are, I think, truly alleged. But were it otherwise; is the judgment of the writers of the New Testament, in interpreting passages of the Old, so connected either with their veracity, or with their means of information concerning what was passing in their own times, as that a critical mistake, even were it clearly made out, should overthrow their historical credit?

Another error imputed to the first Christians was the expected approach of the day of judgment. I would introduce this objection by a remark upon what appears to me a somewhat similar example. Our Saviour, speaking to Peter of John, said, "If I will that he tarry till I come, what is that to thee?" (John xxi. 22.) These words we find had been so misconstrued, as that a report from thence "went abroad among the brethren, that that disciple should not die." Suppose that this had come down to us amongst the prevailing opinions of the early Christians, and that the particular circumstance from which the mistake sprang had been lost, some, at this day, would have been ready to regard the error as an impeachment of the whole Christian system. Yet with how little justice such a presumption would have been taken up, the information which we happen to possess enables us now to perceive. To those who think that the Scriptures lead us to believe that the early Christians, and even the apostles, expected the approach of the day of judgment in their own times, the same reflection will occur as that which we have made with respect to the error concerning the duration of Saint John's life.

The difficulty which attends the subject of the present chapter is contained in this question; If we once admit the fallibility of the apostolic judgment, in what can we rely upon it? Give me the apostles' testimony, and I do not stand in need of their judgment; give me the facts, and I have complete security for every conclusion I want.

But, although I think that it is competent to the Christian apologist to return this answer, I do not think that it is the only answer which the objection is capable of receiving. The two following cautions, founded in the most reasonable distinctions, will exclude all uncertainty upon this head which can be attended with danger.

First, to separate what was the object of the apostolic mission, and declared by them to be so, from what was extraneous to it. Of points clearly extraneous to the religion nothing need be said. Of points incidentally connected with it something may be added. Demoniacal possession is one of these points. Even they who think it was a general, but erroneous opinion of those times; and that the writers of the New Testament, in common with other Jewish writers of that age, fell into the manner of thinking upon the subject which then universally prevailed, need not be alarmed by the concession, as though they had anything to fear from it for the truth of Christianity. The doctrine was not what Christ brought into the world. It appears in the Christian records as being the subsisting opinion of the age and country in which his ministry was exercised. It was no part of the object of his revelation.

Secondly, that, in reading the apostolic writings, we distinguish between their doctrines and their arguments. Their doctrines came to them by revelation properly so called; yet in propounding these doctrines in their writings or discourses they were wont to illustrate, support, and enforce them by such analogies, arguments, and considerations as their own thoughts suggested. Thus the admission of the Gentiles to the Christian profession without a previous subjection to the law of Moses, was imported to the apostles by revelation, and was attested by the miracles which attended the Christian ministry among them. The apostles' own assurance of the matter rested upon this foundation. Nevertheless, Saint Paul, when treating of the subject, often a great variety of topics in its proof and vindication. The doctrine itself must be received: but it is not necessary, in order to defend Christianity, to defend the validity of every argument which the apostle has brought into the discussion.

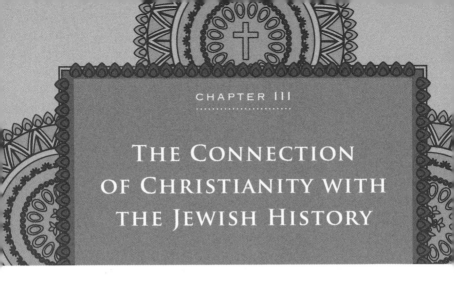

## CHAPTER III

# THE CONNECTION
# OF CHRISTIANITY WITH
# THE JEWISH HISTORY

Undoubtedly our Saviour assumes the divine origin of the Mosaic institution: and, independently of his authority, I conceive it to be very difficult to assign any other cause for the commencement or existence of that institution.

Undoubtedly, also, our Saviour recognises the prophetic character of many of their ancient writers. So far, therefore, we are bound as Christians to go. But to make Christianity answerable, with its life, for the circumstantial truth of each separate passage of the Old Testament, the genuineness of every book, the information, fidelity, and judgment of every writer in it, is to bring unnecessary difficulties into the whole system. These books were universally read and received by the Jews of our Saviour's time. He and his apostles, in common with all other Jews, referred to them, alluded to them, used them. Yet, except where he expressly ascribes a divine authority to particular predictions, I do not know that we can strictly draw any conclusion from the books being so used and applied, beside the proof of their notoriety and reception at that time. In this view, our Scriptures afford a valuable testimony to those of the Jews.

A reference in the New Testament to a passage in the Old does not so fix its authority as to exclude all inquiry into its credibility, or into the separate reasons upon which that credibility is founded.

I have thought it necessary to state this point explicitly, because a fashion, revived by Voltaire, and pursued by the disciples of his school, seems to have much prevailed of late,* of attacking Christianity through the sides of Judaism. Some objections of this class are founded in misconstruction, some in exaggeration; but all proceed upon a supposition that the attestation which the Author and first teachers of Christianity gave to the divine mission of Moses and the prophets extends to every point and portion of the Jewish history; and so extends as to make Christianity responsible, in its own credibility, for the circumstantial truth of every narrative contained in the Old Testament.

---

* [This is referring to the 1850s.]

W e acknowledge that the Christian religion, although it converted great numbers, did not produce an universal, or even a general conviction in the minds of men of the age and countries in which it appeared. And this want of a more complete success has been thought by some to form a strong objection to the reality of the facts which the history contains.

The matter of the objection divides itself into two parts; as it relates to the Jews, and as it relates to Heathen nations: because the minds of these two descriptions of men may have been, with respect to Christianity, under the influence of very different causes.

Now upon the subject of the truth of the Christian religion; with us there is but one question, viz., whether the miracles were actually wrought? From acknowledging the miracles, we pass instantaneously to the acknowledgment of the whole. If we believe the works of any one of them, we believe in Jesus. Yet it appears to me perfectly certain, that the state of thought in the mind of a Jew of our Saviour's age was totally different from this. After allowing the reality of the miracle, he had a great deal to do to persuade himself that Jesus was the Messiah. It appears that the miracles did not irresistibly carry even those who saw them to the conclusion intended to be drawn from them; or so compel assent, as to leave no room for suspense, for the exercise of candour, or the effects of prejudice. And to this point, at least, the evangelists may be allowed to be good witnesses; because it is a point in which exaggeration or disguise would have been the other way.

"Believing in Jesus" was not only to believe that he wrought miracles, but that he was the Messiah. With us there is no difference between these two things; with them there was the greatest.

In the next chapter, we have a reflection of the evangelist entirely suited to this state of the case: "But though he had done so many miracles before them, yet believed they not on him." (Chap. xii. 37.) The evangelist does not mean to impute the defect of their belief to any doubt about the miracles, but to their not perceiving, the infallible attestation which the works of Jesus bore to the truth of his pretensions.

The ninth chapter of Saint John's Gospel contains a very circumstantial account of the cure of a blind man; a miracle submitted to all the scrutiny and examination which a sceptic could propose. The account contains also a very curious conference between the Jewish rulers and the patient, in which the point for our present notice is, their resistance of the force of the miracle, and of the conclusion to which it led, after they had failed in discrediting its evidence. "We know that God spake unto Moses, but as for this fellow, we know not whence he is." That was the answer which set their minds at rest. In the mind of the poor man restored to sight, which was under no such bias, the miracle had its natural operation. "Herein," says he, "is a marvellous thing, that ye know not from whence he is, yet he hath opened mine eyes. Now we know that God heareth not sinners: but if any man be a worshipper of God, and doeth his will, him he heareth. Since the world began, was it not heard, that any man opened the eyes of one that was born blind. If this man were not of God, he could do nothing." We do not find that the Jewish rulers had any other reply to make to this defence, than that which authority is sometimes apt to make to argument, "Dost thou teach us?"

If it shall be inquired how a turn of thought, so different from what prevails at present, should obtain currency with the ancient Jews; the answer is found in two opinions which are proved to have subsisted in that age and country. The one was their expectation of a Messiah of a kind totally contrary to what the appearance of Jesus bespoke him to be; the other, their persuasion of the agency of demons in the production of supernatural effects. And I think that these two opinions conjointly afford an explanation of their conduct. The first put them upon seeking out some excuse to themselves for not receiving Jesus in the character in which he claimed to be received; and the second supplied them with just such an excuse as they wanted. Let Jesus work what miracles he would, still the answer was in readiness, "that he wrought them by the assistance of Beelzebub." And to this answer no reply could be made, but that which our Saviour did make, by showing that the tendency of his mission was so adverse to the views with which this being was, by the objectors themselves, supposed to act, that it could not reasonably be supposed that he would assist in carrying it on.

II. The infidelity of the Gentile world, and that more especially of men of rank and learning in it, is resolvable into a principle which will account for the inefficacy of any argument or any evidence whatever, viz. contempt prior to examination. The state of religion amongst the Greeks and Romans had a natural tendency to induce this disposition. Dionysius Halicarnassensis remarks, that there were six hundred different kinds of religions or sacred rites exercised at Rome. (Jortin's Remarks on Eccl. Hist. Vol. i. p. 371.) The superior classes of the community treated them all as fables. Can we wonder, then, that Christianity was included in the number, without inquiry into its separate merits? The religion had nothing in its character which immediately engaged their notice. What is said of Jesus Christ, of his nature, office, and ministry, would be in the highest degree alien from the conceptions of their theology. What knew they of grace, of redemption, of justification, of the blood of Christ shed for the sins of men, of reconcilement, of mediation? Christianity was made up of points they had never thought of; of terms which they had never heard.

It was presented also to the imagination of the learned Heathen under additional disadvantage, by reason of its connexion with Judaism. The Jews were ridiculed for being a credulous race; so that whatever reports of a miraculous nature came out of that country were looked upon by the Heathen world as false and frivolous. When they heard of Christianity, they heard of it as a quarrel amongst this people about some articles of their own superstition.

Yet Christianity was still making its way: and, amidst so many impediments to its progress, its actual success is more to be wondered at, than that it should not have opened for itself a passage to the hearts and understandings of the scholars of the age.

And the cause for the rejection of Christianity by men of rank and learning among the Heathens, namely, a strong antecedent contempt, accounts also for their silence concerning it. If they had rejected it upon examination, they would have written about it. Whereas, what men repudiate from a settled contempt of the subject, they do not naturally write books about, or notice much in what they write upon other subjects.

The letters of the younger Pliny furnish an example of this silence, and the cause of it. From his celebrated correspondence with Trajan, we know that the Christian religion prevailed in the province over which he presided; that he had inquired into the matter just so much as a Roman magistrate might be expected to inquire. But although Pliny had viewed Christianity in a nearer position than most of his learned countrymen, yet in more than two hundred and forty letters, the subject is never once again mentioned.

The name and character which Tacitus has given to Christianity, "cxitiabilis superstitio" (a pernicious superstition), and by which he disposes of the whole question of the merits of the religion, afford a strong proof how little he concerned himself to know, about the matter.

Upon the words of Tacitus we may build the following observations:

First; That we are well warranted in calling the view under which the learned men of that age beheld Christianity an obscure and distant view. Had Tacitus known more of Christianity, he would have described the religion differently, though he had rejected it. The "superstition" of the Christians consisted in worshipping a person unknown to the Roman calendar; and the "perniciousness" with which they were reproached was their opposition to the established polytheism.

Secondly; We may from hence remark how little reliance can be placed upon the most acute judgments in subjects which they are pleased to despise; and which they consider as unworthy to be inquired into.

Thirdly; That this contempt, prior to examination, is an intellectual vice, from which the greatest faculties of mind are not free. This habit of thought is extremely dangerous; and more apt than almost any other disposition to produce hasty and contemptuous, and, by consequence, erroneous judgments, both of persons and opinions.

Fourthly; We need not be surprised at many writers of that age not mentioning Christianity at all, when they who did mention it appear to have entirely misconceived its nature and character; and, in consequence, regarded it with contempt.

To the knowledge of the greatest part of the learned heathens, the facts of the Christian history could only come by report. The books, probably, they had never looked into.

I think it by no means unreasonable to suppose that the heathen public were divided into two classes; these who despised Christianity beforehand, and those who received it. In correspondency with which division of character the writers of that age would also be of two classes; those who were silent about Christianity, and those who were Christians. "A good man, who attended sufficiently to the Christian affairs, would become a Christian; after which his testimony ceased to be pagan and became Christian." (Hartley, Obs. p. 119.)

I must also add that the notion of magic was resorted to by the heathen adversaries of Christianity. Justin Martyr alleges this as his reason for arguing from prophecy rather than from miracles. Origen imputes this evasion to Celsus; Jerome to Porphyry; and Lactantius to the heathen in general. It being difficult, however, to ascertain in what degree this notion prevailed, another, and I think an adequate, cause has been assigned for their infidelity.

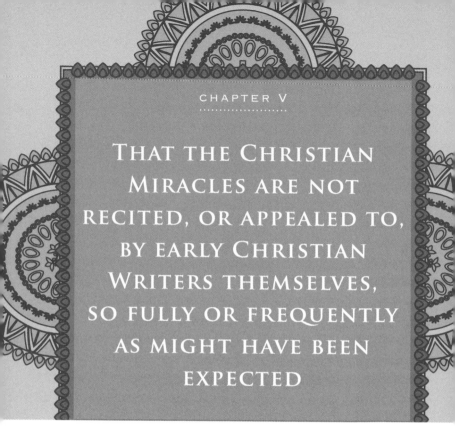

# THAT THE CHRISTIAN MIRACLES ARE NOT RECITED, OR APPEALED TO, BY EARLY CHRISTIAN WRITERS THEMSELVES, SO FULLY OR FREQUENTLY AS MIGHT HAVE BEEN EXPECTED

The epistles of the apostles are either hortatory or argumentative.

So far as these epistles are argumentative, the nature of the argument accounts for the infrequency of these allusions. These epistles were not written to prove the truth of Christianity. The subject was not that which the miracles decided; but it was that which the miracles did not decide, the nature of his person, the design of his advent, its effects, and of those effects the value, kind, and extent. Still I maintain that miraculous evidence lies at the bottom of the argument. For nothing could be so preposterous as for the disciples of Jesus to dispute his office or character; unless they believed that he had shown, by supernatural proofs, that there was something extraordinary in both. Miraculous evidence, therefore if it be incidentally appealed to, it is exactly so much as ought take place, supposing the history to be true.

I would add, that the apostolic epistles resemble the apostolic speeches, which speeches are given by a writer who distinctly records numerous miracles wrought by these apostles themselves, and by the Founder of the institution in their presence; that it is unwarrantable to contend that the infrequency of such recitals in the speeches of the apostles negatives the existence of the miracles, when the speeches are given in immediate conjunction with the history of those miracles: and that a conclusion which cannot be inferred from the speeches without contradicting the whole tenour of the book which contains them cannot be inferred from letters, which in this respect are similar only to the speeches.

The general observation which has been made upon the apostolic writings, namely, that the subject of which they treated did not lead them to any direct recital of the Christian history, belongs to the writings of the apostolic fathers. The epistle of Barnabas is much like the epistle to the Hebrews; an allegorical application of divers passages of the Jewish history, of their law and ritual, to those parts of the Christian dispensation in which the author perceived a resemblance. The epistle of Clement was written for the sole purpose of quieting certain dissensions that had arisen amongst the members of the church of Corinth; and quotes neither the Old Testament nor the New. The epistles of Polycarp and Ignatius had for their principal object the order and discipline of the churches which they addressed. Yet, under all these circumstances of disadvantage, the great points of the Christian history are fully recognised. This hath been shown in its proper place. (Vide supra, pp. 48–51. [Part 1, Chapter 8])

There is, however, another class of writers to whom the answer above given does not apply; and that is the class of ancient apologists. It is necessary, therefore, to inquire how the matter of the objection stands in these.

The most ancient apologist of whose works we have the smallest knowledge is Quadratus. Quadratus presented his apology to the Emperor Adrian. From a passage of this work it appears that the author did directly and formally appeal to the miracles of Christ: "The works of our Saviour were always conspicuous, for they were real: both they that were healed, and they that were raised from the dead, were seen, not only when they were healed or raised, but for a long time afterwards; not only whilst he dwelled on this earth, but also after his departure, and for a good while after it; insomuch as that some of them have reached to our times," (Euseb. Hist. I. iv. c. 3.)

Justin Martyr, the next of the Christian apologists, whose work is not lost, asserts the performance of miracles by Christ. In his first apology, (Apolog. prim. p. 48, ib.) Justin expressly assigns the reason for his having recourse to the argument from prophecy, rather than miracles; which reason was, that the persons with whom he contended would ascribe these miracles to magic; "lest any of our opponents should say, What hinders, but that he who is called Christ by us, being a man sprung from men, performed the miracles which we attribute to him by magical art?" The suggestion of this reason meets the very point of the present objection. Irenaeus, who came about forty years after him, notices the same evasion in the adversaries of Christianity, and replies to it by the same argument. Lactantius, who lived a century lower, delivers the same sentiment upon the same occasion. v. 3.)

But to return to the Christian apologists in their order. Tertullian:—"That person whom the Jews had vainly imagined, from the meanness of his appearance, to be a mere man, they afterwards, in consequence of the power he exerted, considered as a magician, when he, with one word, ejected devils out of the bodies of men, gave sight to the blind, cleansed the leprous, strengthened the nerves of those that had the palsy, and lastly, with one command, restored the dead to life; when he, I say, made the very elements obey him, assuaged the storms, walked upon the seas, demonstrating himself to be the Word of God." (Tertul. Apolos. p. 20; ed. Priorii, Par. 1675.)

Next in the catalogue of professed apologists we may place Origen. We meet with the old solution of magic applied to the miracles of Christ by the adversaries of the religion. "Celsus," saith Origen, "well knowing what great works may be alleged to have been done by Jesus, pretends to grant that the things related of him are true; such as healing diseases, raising the dead, feeding multitudes with a few loaves, of which large fragments were left." (Orig. cont. Cels. lib. ii. sect. 48.) And then Celsus gives, it seems, an answer to these proofs of our Lord's mission, which, as Origen understood it, resolved the phenomena into magic; for Origen begins his reply by observing, "You see that Celsus in a manner allows that there is such a thing as magic." (Lardner's Jewish and Heath. Test, vol. ii. p. 294, ed. 4to.)

This magic, these demons, by which many of that age accounted for the Christian miracles, and which answers the advocates of Christianity often thought it necessary to refute by arguments drawn particularly from prophecy. That such reasons were ever seriously urged and seriously received, is only a proof what a gloss and varnish fashion can give to any opinion.

It appears, therefore, that the miracles of Christ, understood in their literal and historical sense, were positively and precisely asserted and appealed to by the apologists for Christianity; which answers the allegation of the objection.

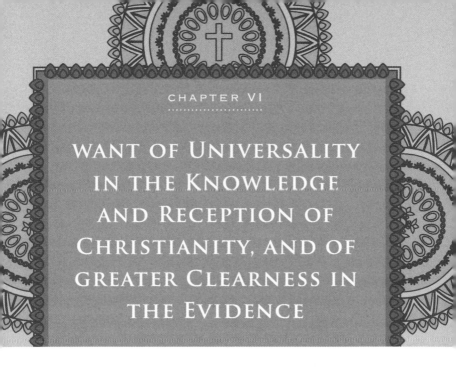

# WANT OF UNIVERSALITY IN THE KNOWLEDGE AND RECEPTION OF CHRISTIANITY, AND OF GREATER CLEARNESS IN THE EVIDENCE

The advocates of Christianity do not deny that it be within the compass of divine power to have communicated to the world a higher degree of assurance, and to have given to his communication a stronger and more extensive influence.

The question is, not whether Christianity possesses the highest possible degree of evidence, but whether the not having more evidence be a sufficient reason for rejecting that which we have.

Throughout that order of nature, we find a system of beneficence: we are seldom or never able to make out a system of optimism. There are few cases in which we cannot suppose something more perfect than what we see. The rain is confessedly amongst the contrivances of the Creator for the sustentation of the animals and vegetables which subsist upon the surface of the earth. Yet how partially: and irregularly is it supplied! We could imagine showers to fall just where and when they would do good; always seasonable, everywhere sufficient. Yet, does the seeming inferiority of the one to the other, authorise us to say, that the present disposition of the atmosphere is not amongst the productions of the Deity? The observation which we have exemplified in the single instance of the rain of heaven may be repeated concerning most of the phenomena of nature; and the true conclusion to which it leads is that to inquire what the Deity might have done, and to build any propositions upon such inquiries against evidence of facts, is wholly unwarrantable. Christianity participates of this character. The true similitude between nature and revelation consists in this—that they each bear strong marks of their original, that they each also bear appearances of irregularity and defect. A system of strict optimism may be the real system in both cases. But what I contend is that we ought not to expect to perceive that in revelation which we hardly perceive in anything; that beneficence, of which, we can judge, ought to satisfy us that optimism, of which we cannot judge, ought not to be sought after.

The existence of Deity is left to be collected from observations, which every man, perhaps, is not capable of making. Can it be argued that God does not exist because if he did, he would let us see him, or discover himself to man kind by proofs which no inadvertency could miss, no prejudice withstand?

The Deity hath not touched the order of nature in vain. The Jewish religion produced great and permanent effects; the Christian religion hath done the same. It hath disposed the world to amendment. It is by no means improbable that it may become universal; and that the world may continue in that stage so long as that the duration of its reign may bear a vast proportion to the time of its partial influence.

What would be the real effect of that overpowering evidence which our adversaries require in a revelation it is difficult foretell. Some consequences would, it is probable, attend this economy, which do not befit a revelation from God. One is, that irresistible proof would not answer the purpose of trial and probation; would call for no exercise of candour, seriousness, humility, inquiry, no submission of passion, interests, and prejudices, to moral evidence and to probable truth; no habits of reflection; none of that previous desire to learn and to obey the will of God, which forms perhaps the test of the virtuous principle, and which induces men to attend to every credible intimation of that will, and to resign present advantages and present pleasures to every reasonable expectation of propitiating his favour.

II. These modes of communication would leave no place for the admission of internal evidence; which ought to bear a part in the proof of every revelation, because it is a species of evidence which applies itself to the knowledge, love, and practice, of virtue, and which operates in proportion to the degree of those qualities which it finds in the person whom it addresses. Men of good dispositions, amongst Christians, are greatly affected by the impression which the Scriptures themselves make upon their minds. Their conviction is much strengthened by these impressions. And this perhaps was intended to be one effect to be produced by the religion. It is likewise true, to whatever cause we ascribe it, that they who sincerely endeavour to act, according to what they believe, and according to a rational estimate of consequences, and, above all, according to the just effect of those principles of gratitude and devotion which even the view of nature generates in a well-ordered mind, seldom fail of proceeding farther. This also may have been exactly what was designed.

Whereas, may it not be said that irresistible evidence would confound all characters and all dispositions? would subvert rather than promote the true purpose of the Divine counsels; which is, not to produce obedience by a force little short of mechanical constraint, but to treat moral agents agreeably to what they are? "It is not meet to govern rational free agents in via by sight and sense. It would be no trial or thanks to the most sensual wretch to forbear sinning, if heaven and hell were open to his sight. That spiritual vision and fruition is our state in patria." (Baxter's Reasons, p. 357.) Few things are more improbable than that the human species should be the highest order of beings in the universe. If there be classes above us of rational intelligences, clearer manifestations may belong to them. And it may be one to which we ourselves hereafter shall attain.

III. But may it not also be asked, whether the perfect display of a future state of existence would be compatible with the success of human affairs? I can easily conceive that this impression may be overdone; that it may so seize the thoughts as to leave no place for the cares and offices of men's several stations, no anxiety for worldly prosperity, or even for a worldly provision, and, by consequence, no sufficient stimulus to secular industry. Of the first Christians we read, "that all that believed were together, and had all things common; and sold their possessions and goods, and parted them to all men, as every man had need; and continuing daily with one accord in the temple, and breaking bread from house to house, did eat their meat with gladness and singleness of heart" (Acts ii. 44–46.) This was just what might be expected from miraculous evidence coming with full force upon the senses of mankind: but I much doubt whether, if this state of mind had been universal, or long-continued, the business of the world could have gone on. Agriculture, manufactures, trade, and navigation, would not, I think, have flourished, if they could have been exercised at all. Men would have addicted themselves to contemplative and ascetic lives, instead of lives of business and of useful industry.

By the manner in which the religion is now proposed, a great portion of the human species is enabled and of these multitudes of every generation are induced, to seek and effectuate their salvation through the medium of Christianity, without interruption of the prosperity or of the regular course of human affairs.

## CHAPTER VII

# SUPPOSED EFFECTS OF CHRISTIANITY

That a religion which holds forth the final reward of virtue and punishment of vice, and proposes those distinctions of virtue and vice which the wisest part of mankind confess to be just, should not be believed, is very possible; but that, so far as it is believed, it should not produce any good, but rather a bad effect upon public happiness, is a proposition which it requires very strong evidence to render credible. Yet many have been found to contend for this paradox.

In the conclusions, however, which these writers draw from what they call experience, two sources, I think, of mistake may be perceived.

One is, that they look for the influence of religion in the wrong place.

The other, that they charge Christianity with many consequences for which it is not responsible.

I. The influence of religion is not to be sought for in the councils of princes, in the debates or resolutions of popular assemblies, in the conduct of governments towards their subjects, of states and sovereigns towards one another; of conquerors at the head of their armies, or of parties intriguing for power at home; but must be perceived in the silent course of private and domestic life. Even there its influence may not be very obvious to observation. The kingdom of heaven is within us. That which the substance of the religion, its hopes and consolation, its intermixture with the thoughts, the devotion of the heart, the control of appetite, the steady direction of will to the commands of God, is necessarily invisible. Yet these depend the virtue and the happiness of millions. Religion operates most upon those of whom history knows the least; upon fathers and mothers, their families, upon orderly tradesman, the quiet villager, the manufacturer at his loom, the husbandman in his fields. It cannot be thought strange that this influence should elude the grasp and touch of public history; for what is public history but register of the successes and disappointments, the vices, the follies, and the quarrels, of those who engage in contentions power?

The Christian religion also acts upon public usages and institutions, by an operation which is only secondary and indirect. Christianity can only reach public institutions through private character. Now its influence upon private character may be considerable, yet many public usages and institutions repugnant to its principles may remain. To get rid of these, the reigning part of the community must act together. It has mitigated the conduct of war, and the treatment of captives. It has softened the administration of despotic governments. It has abolished polygamy. It has restrained the licentiousness of divorces. It has put an end to the exposure of children and the immolation of slaves. It has banished, if not unnatural vices, at least the toleration of them. In all countries in which it is professed it has produced numerous establishments for the relief of sickness and poverty; and in some, a regular and general provision by law.

The benefit of religion, being felt chiefly in the obscurity of private stations, necessarily escapes the observation of history. From the first general notification of Christianity to the present day, there have been in every age many millions, whose names were never heard of, made better by it, not only in their conduct, but in their disposition; and happier, in that which alone deserves the name of happiness, the tranquillity and consolation of their thoughts. It has been since its commencement the author of happiness and virtue to millions and millions of the human race.

Christianity also, in every country in which it is professed, hath obtained a sensible, although not a complete influence upon the public judgment of morals. And this is very important. For without the occasional correction which public opinion receives, by referring to some fixed standard of morality, no man can foretel into what extravagances it might wander. In this way it is possible that many may be kept in order by Christianity who are not themselves Christians. They may be guided by the rectitude which it communicates to public opinion.

After all, the value of Christianity is not to be appreciated by its temporal effects. The object of revelation is to influence human conduct in this life; but what is gained to happiness by that influence can only be estimated by taking in the whole of human existence. Then, as hath already been observed, there may be also great consequences of Christianity which do not belong to it as a revelation. The effects upon human salvation of the mission, of the death, of the present, of the future agency of Christ, may be universal, though the religion be not universally known.

Secondly, I assert that Christianity is charged with many consequences for which it is not responsible. I believe that religious motives have had no more to do in the formation of nine tenths of the intolerant and persecuting laws which in different countries have been established upon the subject of religion, than they have had to do in England with the making of the game-laws. These measures, although they have the Christian religion for their subject, are resolvable into a principle which Christianity certainly did not plant, which principle is that they who are in possession of power do what they can to keep it. Christianity is answerable for no part of the mischief which has been brought upon the world by persecution. Had there been in the New Testament, what there are in the Koran, precepts authorising coercion in the propagation of the religion, and the use of violence towards unbelievers, the case would have been different. This distinction could not have been taken, nor this defence made.

If it be objected, as I apprehend it will be, that Christianity is chargeable with every mischief of which it has been the occasion, though not the motive; I answer that, if the malevolent passions be there, the world will never want occasions. Did the applauded intercommunity of the pagan theology preserve the peace of the Roman world? Was it bigotry that carried Alexander into the East, or brought Caesar into Gaul? Are the nations of the world into which Christianity hath not found its way, or from which it hath been banished, free from contentions? Europe itself has known no religious wars for some centuries, yet has hardly ever been without war. Are the calamities which at this day afflict it to be imputed to Christianity? In order to be a persecutor it is not necessary to be a bigot: in rage and cruelty, in mischief and destruction, fanaticism itself can be outdone by infidelity.

Finally, if war, as it is now carried on between nations produce less misery and ruin than formerly, we are indebted perhaps to Christianity for the change more than to any other cause. Viewed therefore even in its relation to this subject, it appears to have been of advantage to the world. It hath humanised the conduct of wars; it hath ceased to excite them.

## CHAPTER VIII

# CONCLUSION

In religion, as in every other subject of human reasoning, much depends upon the order in which we dispose our inquiries.

The rational way of treating a subject of such acknowledged importance is, to attend, in the first place, to the general and substantial truth of its principles, and to that alone. When we once perceive a ground of credibility in its history; we shall proceed with safety to inquire into the interpretation of its records, and into the doctrines which have been deduced from them.

This conduct of the understanding will uphold personal Christianity, even in those countries in which it is established under forms the most liable to difficulty and objection. What is clear in Christianity we shall find to be sufficient, and to be infinitely valuable; what is dubious, unnecessary to be decided, or of very subordinate importance, and what is most obscure, will teach us to bear with the opinions which others may have formed upon the same subject.

A judgment, moreover, which is once pretty well satisfied of the general truth of the religion will not only thus discriminate in its doctrines, but will possess sufficient strength to overcome the reluctance of the imagination to admit articles of faith which are attended with difficulty of apprehension, if such articles of faith appear to be truly parts of the revelation. It was to be expected beforehand, that what related to the economy and to the persons of the invisible world, which revelation profess to do, should contain some points remote from the comprehension of a mind which hath acquired all its ideas from sense and from experience.

It hath been my care in the preceding work to preserve the separation between evidences and doctrines as inviolable as I could; to remove from the primary question all considerations which have been unnecessarily joined with it; and to offer a defence to Christianity which every Christian might read without seeing the tenets in which he had been brought up attacked or decried: few or none of our many controversies with one another affect or relate to the proofs of our religion.

The truth of Christianity depends upon its leading facts, and upon them alone. Now of these we have evidence which ought to satisfy us, at least until it appear that mankind have ever been deceived by the same. We have some uncontested and incontestable points, to which the history of the human species hath nothing similar to offer. A Jewish peasant changed the religion of the world, and that without force, without power, without support; without one natural source or circumstance of attraction, influence, or success. Such a thing hath not happened in any other instance.

But whether these or any other attempts to satisfy the imagination bear any resemblance to the truth; or whether the imagination, which, as I have said before, is the mere slave of habit, can be satisfied or not; when a future state, and the revelation of a future state is not only perfectly consistent with the attributes of the Being who governs the universe; but when it is more; when it alone removes the appearance of contrariety which attends the operations of his will towards creatures capable of comparative merit and demerit, of reward and punishment; when a strong body of historical evidence, confirmed by many internal tokens of truth and authenticity, gives us just reason to believe that such a revelation hath actually been made; we ought to set our minds at rest that in the resources of Creative Wisdom expedients cannot be wanted to carry into effect what the Deity hath purposed: that either a new and mighty influence will descend upon the human world to resuscitate extinguished consciousness; or that, amidst the other wonderful contrivances with which the universe abounds, and by some of which we see animal life, in many instances, assuming improved forms of existence, acquiring new organs, new perceptions, and new sources of enjoyment, provision is also made, though by methods secret to us, for conducting the objects of God's moral government, through the necessary changes of their frame, to those final distinctions of happiness and misery which he hath declared to be reserved for obedience and transgression, for virtue and vice, for the use and the neglect, the right and the wrong employment of the faculties and opportunities with which he hath been pleased, severally, to intrust and to try us.